# SEARCHING FOR THE MEANING OF LIFE

# Searching

## for the

# Meaning of Life

*Studies in the Book of Ecclesiastes*

**Paul Earnhart**

*Searching for the Meaning of Life: Studies in the Book of Ecclesiastes*
© 2018 by DeWard Publishing Company, Ltd.
P.O. Box 6259, Chillicothe, Ohio 45601
800.300.9778
**www.deward.com**

Cover design by Evangela Creative.

Reasonable care has been taken to trace original sources for any excerpts and quotations appearing in this book and to document such information. For material not in the public domain, fair-use standards and practices were followed. Should any attribution be found to be incorrect or incomplete, the publisher welcomes written documentation supporting correction for subsequent printings.

Printed in the United States of America.

ISBN: 978-1-947929-00-5

# Contents

# The Preacher's Purpose

The purpose of the writer of Ecclesiastes is to reflect upon his own futile efforts to find ultimate meaning and purpose amidst life's perplexities, and to warn those who would come after him (especially the young, 12.1) that nothing "under the sun" will ever fulfill the eternal longing which God has put in the heart of man (3.11). It is for this reason that he assumes the role of the Preacher (Qoheleth), or one who calls together or addresses an assembly (thus, from Greek, Ecclesiastes (*ekklesia*, assembly). Yet it is evident that Solomon views his counsel, not as mere prudent advice, but as "words of truth … given by one Shepherd" (12.10–11). The words of this book are from God.

The pronouncements that Solomon makes about life will seem wholly erroneous and even exceedingly cynical unless we remember that he is speaking of life as viewed from beneath the sun. From this vantage point the observations of the Preacher are eminently valid in a world that gives no clue as to life's purpose, provides no answer to man's ultimate longing, and furnishes no resolution to life's jarring contradictions and inequities. Solomon is simply declaring that man by his unaided wisdom will never penetrate the mystery that guards the purposes of God. He anticipates the words of Paul that God in His wisdom has determined that man by his wisdom would never know Him (1 Cor 1.21). The apostle also says that God because of sin subjected the creation to futility (Rom 3.20). Ecclesiastes is simply making these same points but in a more dramatic and specific way. And though the Preacher, unlike the apostle, has no gospel of grace to preach, he does anticipate it, finding the resolution of all things in God.

The purpose of Ecclesiastes seems fairly clear but it does not yield itself to an obvious, clear-cut outline. The book seems to spiral freely and repeatedly through the same themes of the world's bewildering contradictions and frustrations and the confidence that the God who sits above the sun will bring an ultimate resolution. Man finds his center, not in the world of vanity, but in the God of eternity.

In this great book Solomon teaches us two lessons. First, the critical importance of seeking ultimate meaning and fulfillment in the Creator rather than the creation. And then, once having planted our feet firmly in eternity, to find joy in the gifts of God which, however temporary, do bless us in this world beneath the sun.

## 1.1–8: Going Around in Circles

With lean brevity the book begins: "The words of the Preacher, Son of David, king in Jerusalem." "The words" identifies far more than just what the Preacher has to say. It was a well-known expression of Old Testament sages and prophets (Prov 30.1; 31.1; Jer 1.1; Amos 1.1) and bears a remarkable similarity to the introduction to Jeremiah: "The words of Jeremiah, the son of Hilkiah, of the priests who were in Anathoth."

Solomon moves immediately to the thesis which brackets his book: "Vanity of vanities, all is vanity" (1.2; 12.8), then proceeds directly to identify where the pointlessness of life lies: "What profit does a man have from all his labor in which he toils under the sun?," and then begins to demonstrate it. Life is wearisomely pointless due to life's brevity. The earth on which life is played out seems to last forever while we the actors constantly come and go (1.4). Furthermore, even if we could abide like the earth, life under the sun never gets you anywhere because the earth moves endlessly in constantly repeated cycles of sun, wind, and sea (1.4–7). It is the progress of a squirrel cage, motion without direction. Interestingly this was precisely the Greek view of history, that human events kept cycling in a perpetual repetition of the same events (History repeats itself). Traveling in endless circles like a man lost in the snow it became "a tale told by an idiot, signifying nothing." So is life without God. No wonder it is laborious. It goes nowhere and reveals no purpose or point. The heavens may declare God's glory (Psa 19.1) and the creation reveal God's power and deity (Rom 1.20) but there is nothing in the world beneath the sun that speaks of the intent and destiny of life. Without help from above we are left to wander the earth in search of who we are and where we are going. It was the Bible which gave the world a view of history that was linear, purposeful, moving to a consummation like an arrow hurtling to its target.

The world as seen from under the sun, because of its endless, meaningless cycling, is inexpressibly wearisome. In spite of all our arduous labor our brief sojourn upon the earth satisfies neither eye nor ear (1.8) nor heart. Solomon's sense of vanity is not mere emptiness or futility but "vanity of vanities," futility of the profoundest sort, an emptiness that reaches to the very essence of life.

# Nothing New Under the Sun

Solomon's conclusion to the prologue of Ecclesiastes (1.9–11), though not cynical, does seem to be filled with despair. We are so accustomed to placing the template of revelation over the face of creation that we easily lose the true sense of meaninglessness which life under the sun can seem to reflect. The effort of some to explain Solomon's conclusions as those of a man who lived before the gospel are beside the point since he is looking at the world from "beneath the sun" where human effort and human wisdom struggle to make sense of things apart from God.

We need to keep reminding ourselves that although God has not left Himself without some witness in the material universe (Acts 14.15–17; 17.28–29; Rom 1.20), it still appears by mere observation to be exactly what Solomon said of it—an endless cycle of unchanging patterns and insoluble problems. Even the gospel which brings true purpose and hope into the world beneath the sun still leaves some mysteries to be dealt with by sheer trust in the wisdom and grace of God (Deut 29.29). The book of Job is a powerful treatment of this truth.

"And there is nothing new under the sun" (1.9). From the vantage point of our vaunted technology we are inclined to challenge this statement. Was Solomon able to fly? Did any of his contemporaries set foot on the moon? Did he understand nuclear physics? But we are too short-sighted. Look more deeply, as Solomon did.

Have the rotations of the earth or the cycles of nature been altered? Have the heavens been changed; have the stars fallen from the sky (Isa 40.26)? Do we not look at the same constellations, moving in the same courses, that that ancient Israelite did? In the final analysis all our science has had about as much essential effect on the world under the sun as a gnat dropping an eyelash. For all of humanity's parading up and down everything has been left as the Creator made it. And not only that but the basic problems of humanity remain the same. Like the very first man we still struggle with the demons of ignorance, guilt and mortality.

"Is there anything of which it may be said,' See this is new'? It has already been in ancient times before us" (1.10). The endless cycling of the universe is reflected in the affairs of man as he seeks closure on something ultimate. There, too, there is nothing new— no evidence of conclusion, direction, or purpose. We have filled history with sound and fury but altered nothing for all our labor. It is this very theme that Solomon is still pressing as the book ends: "Of the making of many books there is no end and much study is wearisome to the flesh" (12.12).

Some have said that the Preacher's view is only valid if God is left out of the picture because it sees the world as a closed system where miracles and divine providence are precluded. But as we have stated that is precisely Solomon's perspective—the world "under the sun" where man seeks by his own unaided wisdom to find understanding and meaning. The question which introduces this section is not about the labor of God but the labor of man: "What profit has a man from all his labor which he toils under the sun?" (1.3). He is not inquiring about what God has done from above to give life meaning, but about what of true profit man can find by his own labor and wisdom in the world beneath the sun. It is not fair therefore to array against Solomon Peter's denunciation of ungodly scoffers who would ridicule the idea of divine judgment on the basis of an unchanging creation (2 Pet 3.3–7). The Preacher, who sees God as creator, lawgiver and judge (12.1, 13, 14), would have agreed with Peter. Solomon is simply saying that man as a race has neither produced or found anything new: He has simply run in the same old circles. So it is in a world subjected to futility where men groan for that which that world cannot supply (Rom 8.20–22).

The Preacher's conclusion is based upon his premise. If nothing changes, nothing can be new. And any thought that there is rises from limited knowledge or failed memory. "There is no remembrance of former things, Nor will there be any remembrance of things that are to come by those who will come after" (1.11). As to life under the sun, what is has been, and will be. Simply put, he who has seen the present has seen it all. He cannot keep endlessly hoping that men will finally work some grand resolution of all things and bring human life to ultimate focus. Solomon knew, for he had tried to find the way "beneath the sun" and wretchedly failed. He well knew that all the vanities of this broken world could only come to meaning in the wisdom and will of God. He alone has the power to make all things new (Rev 21.5).

# The Emptiness Of Human Wisdom: *Ecclesiastes 1.12–18*

*"I the Preacher, was king over Israel in Jerusalem. And I set my heart to seek and search out by wisdom concerning all that is done under heaven; this burdensome task God has given to the sons of man, by which they may be exercised" (Ecc 1.12–13).*

There is an evident shift here from general observations about the vanity of the material world to the author's own profound experience of this truth in the affairs of men ("all that is done under the sun"). Solomon now presses his conclusions as the result of a carefully studied effort by one of immense resources (1.12; 1 Kgs 3.13) and unequaled wisdom (1.16; 1 Kgs 3.12). He has learned some hard personal lessons and is determined to share them with his readers.

It is a bit difficult to determine in these verses whether wisdom was the means or end of Solomon's quest. Perhaps, in a sense, it was both. He had hoped by wise research into human affairs to find life's meaning, the true and ultimate wisdom. The wisdom the Preacher exercises in his search is not divine, but human. It comes not by revelation but by observation and experience of life. It is limited to what a man or men can know by their own unaided skills. So the king focused all his intellectual and intuitive powers on a study of life which was both deep (*darash*, penetrating into the depth) and wide (*tur*, extensive search, "all that is done under the sun"). And no one could have done it more thoroughly.

The Preacher characterizes this search for ultimate answers in the world of men and nature not only as a "burdensome task" but one that "God has given to the sons of man." By God's design human beings are driven not just to live but to understand the meaning of life. We are not content just to exist. As Solomon will later put it, "He has put eternity in our hearts..." (3.11). But this agonizes us because the mystery that tantalizes our mind will not yield to its powers. And what is available for us to observe and experience in the affairs of men brings no meaning and no peace. So the Preacher concludes, "I have seen all the works that are done under the sun; and indeed it is vanity and grasping for the wind" (v 14). Like the Cynic Diogenes who went about Athens with a lantern looking in vain for an honest man, Solomon has searched for something ultimately meaningful under the sun and failed to find it.

Yet if Solomon's pursuit of final answers proved fruitless it did serve to emphasize how many things under the sun are intractably crooked and painfully absent. "What is crooked cannot be made straight and what is lacking cannot be numbered" (v 15). He is not speaking here so much of human sinfulness as of the apparent contradictions of what is just, fair and sensible and the missing pieces that make the solving of the puzzle impossible. The reason that God's providence is often so indecipherable arises both from our own limited knowledge and the fact that God Himself has clouded the face of creation by subjecting it to vanity because of human rebellion (Rom 8.20).The world that baffled Solomon was not the world that God had originally created.

The Preacher's failure to find peace in wisdom is but a powerful demonstration of Paul's declaration that "in the wisdom of God the world through wisdom did not know God" (1 Cor 1.21). God, then, has so arranged things under the sun that however much we try to know the infinite mind of deity we cannot. It is a recurrent theme in Ecclesiastes (3.11; 7.23; 8.16–17). The mind of man cannot penetrate the mystery of God's purpose (Rom 11.34). Human philosophy, the effort to do so, has always been a function of human pride (Jas 3.13–15). Like two-year-old children we deny all need of help and stubbornly try to take care of everything for ourselves no matter the awful mess we make of it. True wisdom, not of this world, comes down from God, as might be expected (Jas 3.17–18; Dan 2.20–22), but it will only come to those who humbly confess their ignorance and foolishness (1 Cor 3.18–19). Solomon's quest humbled him. Unfortunately it does not do the same for all.

The Preacher muses as he brings the chronicle of his search for wisdom under the sun to a close (Ecc 1.16–17). He remembers that he had brought to the task greater resolve, skill and understanding than any before him and yet his failure was still absolute. Lesser men should take note that "… in much wisdom is much grief, and he who increases knowledge increases sorrow" (Ecc 1.18). But we are slow to learn. We still dream of penetrating the immense mind of God with our small minds (Stephen Hawking, *A Brief History of Time*, p. 175). The irony is that we struggle futilely to learn what He is freely telling all who have the humility to listen (Eph 3.8–9).

# Of Pleasures and Palaces

*"I said in my heart, 'Come now, I will test you with mirth;*
*therefore enjoy pleasure'; but surely, this also was vanity. I said*
*of laughter—'Madness!'; and of mirth, 'What does it accom-*
*plish?'" (Ecc 2.1–2).*

Solomon, his failed experiment with wisdom having been re-
counted, now tells of a similarly empty attempt to find contentment in pleasure. From the discipline of careful thought
he turns first to a passionate pursuit of the sensual. He pours
himself into every activity pleasing to the senses, bombarding
himself with delights of the flesh. If he could not think his way
to life's purpose, perhaps he could experience his way to it. But
even before he relates the details of his new research he declares
its results—complete and utter madness. It accomplished absolutely nothing.

*"I searched in my heart how to gratify my flesh with wine, while*
*guiding my heart with wisdom, and how to lay hold on folly, till*
*I might see what was good for the sons of men to do under heaven*
*all the days of their lives"* (v 3). It strikes us as strange that the
Preacher should begin intentionally to experiment with "folly"
but this is likely a word used in retrospect. The Hebrew verb
from which its original is formed usually indicates moral and

spiritual stupidity rather than just intellectual foolishness (1 Sam 13.13; 2 Sam 24.10), thus, "the wickedness of folly" (7.25).

Solomon speaks specifically here of gratifying himself with wine. Does he mean to refer to drunkenness (Provs 20.1; 23.29–30; 31.4–5) or simply to the delights of good and nourishing but non-intoxicating food (Ecc 9.7–8)? And is the folly here in immoral excesses or in trying to turn otherwise innocent pleasures (delectable food, pleasing clothing, lovely music; 2:8b) into the whole purpose of life? The Preacher seems very intent on telling us that his experiment with pleasure never led him to mindless excess ("while guiding my heart with wisdom"). Perhaps, practically, it does not matter. Whether one dives headfirst into pleasure or tastes its delights with respectable prudence, neither will bring any ultimate satisfaction. The former may cause more momentary havoc but both will end in emptiness of heart.

This is an important warning for a generation intent on living in a continuous party, entertaining itself into stupefaction. All too soon the endless banqueting grows stale and the laughter dies or becomes hollow (7.6). The pursuit of pleasure is necessarily flawed by its essential selfishness and devaluation of others. It becomes increasingly addictive, increasingly unsatisfying. This is not to disparage innocent fun but building our lives on it is to mindlessly and endlessly relive some sophomoric stage of life.

Solomon refers later in this section (v 8b) to another sensual delight to which he gave himself, "the delights of the sons of men" (NKJV) or as it may be better translated "the pleasures of men— many concubines" (NASB). This may be a case of understatement for the king actually had 700 wives and 300 concubines (1 Kgs 11.3). One wonders how in his relatively short lifetime he ever managed to hold even a brief conversation with each of them! His proverbs suggest that they must have given him as much pain as pleasure (Prov 21.9, 19; 27.15) and they became the primary reason for his apostasy from God (1 Kgs 11.4). Marriage is truly a blessing from God (9.9) but not even a wonderful marriage can bear the load of being life's ultimate purpose! It is evident in this age of serial polygamy that some are still seeking to find transcendent happiness in marriage, running from one partner to the next. None of them will ever approach the level of Solomon's experiment and like him they too will fail. We ought to be wise enough to learn from the other fellow's experience.

But not all pleasure is sensual. *"I made my works great, I built myself houses, and planted myself vineyards. I made myself gardens and orchards, and I planted all kinds of fruit trees in them"* (2.4–5). Failing to find life's meaning in physical gratifications Solomon turns to more substantial and useful pleasures, the creating of great palaces and delightful gardens, the multiplication of great herds and flocks and the accumulation of great wealth. The purpose of all this frenetic building was to somehow bring a sense of fulfillment and peace and compared to his plunge into sensuality it was certainly a step up. Solomon did find pleasure in the midst of his work (2.10) but when it was done and he reflected on its ultimate significance he concluded that it, too, was meaningless (2.11).

Solomon with his virtually limitless resources had restricted himself from no desired pleasure or pursuit (2.10) and it worked to make him surpassingly great among men (2.9). Yet for all his achievements he concluded with an emptiness perhaps even greater than that with which he began. It was destined to fail from the beginning because he was searching in the wrong places and always for the wrong reason—*for himself* (2.4–6, 8). Life is not made of pleasures and palaces.

# When Life Dead-Ends:
## *Ecclesiastes 2.12–26*

*"Then I turned myself to consider wisdom and madness and folly; For what can the man do who succeeds the king?—Only what he has already done" (2.12)*

Solomon had found some considerable joy in the great labors of his search for meaning in the world beneath the heavens, but when they ended and he reflected on their real worth, he concluded painfully that everything was "vanity and grasping for the wind" (v 11).

Now the failure of his research makes him question the value of wisdom itself. There is a note of exhaustion and despair in Solomon's concluding observations (vv 18–23). He hates both his life (v 17) and his labor which now seem toilsome and burdensome (vv 22–23) and makes his days sorrowful (v 23). He had done all that he knew to do, this wisest and richest of men (1.16; 2.8–9), and produced nothing. He had played all his intellectual and material cards yet, all his prudence notwithstanding, nothing had worked. The string had run out. And if Solomon with all his resources and wisdom could not wring some true meaning from life, what hope was there for those with infinitely less opportunity? (v 12).

You would think that those of us who have "come after the king" would learn from his experience but the experiment continues to be repeated endlessly with the same unhappy results. It reminds one of the senseless man who kept rereading the same novel hoping it might end differently. Every new generation sees itself as "more progressive" than the last, always imagining that an "enlightened" age will succeed where former ignorance has failed. Our technological age is no different. But this is not a problem of technology; it is a question of the essential nature of man and the universe. You cannot grow cabbage from lead shot no matter how well you plant it.

Life's purpose cannot be found here. Still Solomon is not quite yet willing to dismiss the wise and prudent life as no better than one spent in foolishness. "Then I saw that wisdom excels folly as light excels darkness. The wise man's eyes are in his head but the fool walks in darkness" (2.13–14a). In the practical day to day affairs of life he still believes and will continue to believe that wisdom is a blessing and mindlessness a curse (4.13; 5.3; 7.1–12; 10.1–17).

**Death is Blind to Wisdom and Foolishness.** The thing that stops the Preacher cold is death. "Yet I myself perceived that the same event happens to them all. So I said in my heart, 'As it happens to the fool, it also happens to me, and why was I then more wise?' Then I said in my heart, 'This also is vanity … And, how does the wise man die? As the fool!'" (2.14b–16).

Wisdom may be useful in this life but it yields no answers to life's vital questions and at last wise men die just like fools, and are just as unremembered. What then, he asks, is the real value of wisdom, or of anything beneath the sun?

Solomon concludes with a vividly remembered sense of exhausted emptiness and despair: "Therefore I hated life because the work that was done under the sun was distressing to me, for all is vanity and grasping for the wind" (2.17). He came to hate the work he had once cherished when he realized that death would leave all his labor in the hands of others, perhaps fools who would bring it to nothing (2.18–20). He was dismayed at the reality we must all face—all that we buy or build here will pass soon enough into the hands of others and none of it will survive. The Preacher will later speak the obvious, spoken first by Job (1.21) and later by Paul (1 Tim 6.7), "As he came from his mother's womb, naked shall he return, to go as he came; and he shall take nothing from his labor which he may carry away in his hand" (5.15). It is foolish to build a house on rented land, and madness to build a life on that which cannot sustain nor fulfill it.

Ecclesiastes is haunted by the reality of death and its apparent blindness to wisdom and foolishness, justice and injustice, righteousness and wickedness. It gives the appearance of an uncaring slaughter. Solomon looks unblinkingly at the world that God had first created in perfection and then subjected to vanity (futility) because of sin (Genesis 3.16–19; Romans 8.20), and calls it what it is—an unfulfilling and baffling place whose contradictions can fill life with despair.

Solomon again concludes that man's quest to find ultimate joy and purpose in things under the sun is hopeless (2.23). Still, though they cannot be the foundation on which life is built, he declares for the first time that they do have value when enjoyed as gifts "from the hand of God" (2.24), and while keeping in mind that nothing can have meaning apart from seeking to be good in His sight (2.25–26).

# Trusting the God Who Sets the Times and Seasons of Our Lives: *Ecclesiastes 3.1–15*

This section of Ecclesiastes is perhaps the best known portion of the book. President John F. Kennedy planned to use this familiar passage in his address in Dallas, Texas where he was suddenly felled by an assassin's bullet. Thus the irony of its words, "To everything there is a season, a time for every purpose under heaven. A time to be born, and a time to die." (3.1–2).

It is obvious that this chapter marks the beginning of a new literary unit. The style changes from prose to poetry and the topic changes from God giving wisdom and joy to God setting the times and seasons of life. The Preacher also turns from his own experiences with life and the lessons learned (1.12–2.26) to what God has done and is doing, and the reason for the baffling mystery of events which hide His providence from human understanding. God does indeed give wisdom, knowledge and joy to the good, but that does not mean that His gift comes without puzzling events that seem to challenge God's benevolence toward those who seek to know and do His will.

It should also be noted that there is a connection between this poem and the one which begins the book (1.4–11). They seem to address the same question from different directions. The earlier poem speaks of the inexorable cycles of nature which God has ordained and seem in their endless repetitions to be going nowhere (1.9–10). They are unchanging. In the same way the divinely set times and seasons of life seem also to reveal no consistent evidence of God's purpose for the creatures He has made in His own image (3.11).

Both poems seem to be concerned with the same rhetorical question which pervades the book, "What profit has a man for all his labor in which he toils under the sun?" (1.3) and "What profit has the worker from that in which he labors?" (3.9). Where, in other words, does one find in all this world's endless revolutions and radically alternating events the labor that will bring lasting benefit? Then each poem is followed by a prose commentary (1.10–11; 3.10–15).

## What Time is it?

The words of the Preacher in Ecclesiastes 3.1—"To everything there is a season, a time for every purpose under heaven"—and the fourteen antitheses which whipsaw through verses two to eight, have sent many interpreters struggling to determine the right time for each of the twenty-eight possibilities. This, I think, is a misguided effort. It is God who determines the presence of all these experiences in human life, not man. They serve as a description of a world that has been divinely consigned to futility (Gen 3.17–19; Rom 8.20). These jarring changes alternate between life and death, the good and the ill, the constructive and the destructive, the sad and the joyous, the peaceful and the warring, the gaining and the losing. Solomon's point is that the whole range of life is beyond human control though by nature we have to share in these activities (3.9). He is not urging us to do things at the right time but illustrating man's helplessness before God's providence. Our actions depend upon times and seasons over which we have no control.

The Preacher is not saying that God has foreordained the exact time and circumstance of every human life, though He certainly could know them. He simply describes the jarring oscillation of events which God has made a part of the human experience. They tell us two things: (1) we do not have absolute control of our circumstances, and (2) we cannot discern God's purpose or understand His providence from the circumstances of our lives.

Still there is in us a longing to see in the events of our lives some evidence of direction and ultimate purpose. It is a desire which God has put in us, yet without the ability to discern an answer in life's conflicting events (3.11). So, is it possible to worship God in these differing seasons? Is it possible to find joy in the midst of our adversity, to find dependence on Him in the midst of failing health? Is it possible to be close to God in ever-changing circumstances? The answer of Ecclesiastes and of the whole of Scripture is an unvarying "Yes".

God is working His eternal purpose in this apparently contradictory world. "He has made everything beautiful [appropriate] in its time" (3.11a). But He has arranged things so that we cannot always see how it is being done. And why has God shrouded His providence in this way? So "that men should fear before Him." (3.14). We must learn at last to trust God in the things which we do not understand. That is the lesson of the book of Job. Faith is indeed the victory which overcomes the world (1 John 5.4). What we know of the wisdom, power and goodness of God must suffice to give us confidence in the faithfulness of His promises. That confidence will get us through many a painful and baffling circumstance. There is no guarantee that our heart will not be broken in this world beneath the sun, but there is absolute assurance that the God in whom we trust will never leave us nor forsake us (Heb 13.5), however it may appear otherwise. We live in a broken world, but we need to be of good cheer because our great Redeemer has overcome the world (John 16.33). The victory we seek and the purpose we long to secure is awaiting us, above the sun.

Meanwhile, though there may be many things in our lives that mystify us, we can rejoice in and be grateful for the good days God gives us, and try to learn the lessons which the days of adversity alone can bring (3.12–13; 7.14; Psa 119.65–72). Let us therefore rest assured that in both our tears and our joys God is working for our eternal good (Rom 8.28).

# God's Righteous Rule vs. "The Real World"

This section of Ecclesiastes gives a perfect demonstration of why it is imperative for God's people to "walk by faith and not by sight" (2 Cor 5.7).

The experiences of life "under the sun" by all human beings combined, much less only one, could never yield an insight sufficient to fully determine God's true character and the purpose which drives his dealings with men (Ecc 3.11; 8.17). The nature of God and His will cannot be penetrated by human wisdom (1 Cor 1.21) but is known only by what He has freely revealed to us (1 Cor 2.7–10).

God has spoken to us (Heb 1.1–2), and what the world we live in seems to be saying about Him and ourselves must always be guided by and even overruled by what He has said. For even if our vision of events in the physical and therefore visible world were complete it would be much too narrow to tell the full story. The God who created and rules the world is invisible (1 Tim 1.17) and it is in that which we cannot see that ultimate and unchanging reality resides (2 Cor 4.18). Impenetrable mysteries will therefore always plague those who refuse to look beyond this "present evil world" (Gal 1.4).

Solomon has already affirmed that in spite of the jarring oscillations of life under the sun God has "made everything beautiful in its time" (3.11). In Ecclesiastes 3.16–4.16 he wrestles with the things which seem to contradict God's overruling providence in the lives of men. The Preacher is involved in a theodicy, an effort to justify the God he believes to be righteous with the unremedied inequities easily observed in human affairs. We should note again before proceeding that only a man who believes in a just God should be tortured by such questions. Agnostics ought to be free of them. One wonders why they are not.

"Moreover I saw under the sun: In the place of judgment, wickedness was there: And in the place of righteousness iniquity was there" (3.16). Solomon first addresses the injustice of the courts, the very place where justice ought to be served. In 4.1 he paints a pathetic picture of the just but helpless poor who are crushed by powerful adversaries indifferent to their tearful appeals. It was not only in Solomon's world that such things happened. They happen today, not only abroad but in this country where "equal protection before the law" is a national ideal. Powerful and wealthy people oppress and at times kill with impunity. Beneath the sun the innocent not only at times suffer justice delayed but justice denied. How, asks Solomon, can we reconcile this with a world that a righteous and holy God is running? It is an old question (Job 16.11–17; Psa 73.1–14; Hag 1.12–13).

Solomon will revisit this question more than once. "I have seen everything in my days of vanity: There is a just man who perishes in his righteousness, and there is a wicked man who prolongs life in his wickedness" (7.15) "There is a vanity which occurs on earth, that there are just men to whom it happens according to the work of the wicked; again, there are wicked men to whom it happens according to the work of the righteous" (8.14).

The Preacher in his answer ascends to the invisible world above the sun and reaches beyond sight to faith. "I said in my heart, 'God shall judge the righteous and the wicked, for there is a time there for every purpose and for every work'" (3.17). With these words he affirms that there is life beyond death in which the Lord God will make all crooked things straight and fill all that is lacking. There is no statute of limitations on divine justice and death will not clear the docket. He will later repeat the same answer even more powerfully and specifically: "Though a sinner does evil a hundred times, and his days are prolonged, yet I surely know that it will be well with those that fear God, who fear before Him. But it will not be well with the wicked; nor will he prolong his days which are as a shadow, because he does not fear God" (8.12–13).

In 3.18–21 Solomon seems to continue his response to the problem raised by injustice tolerated in the world. "I said in my heart, 'Concerning the condition of the sons of men, God tests them, that they may see that they themselves are like animals'" (3.18). Here he answers the naturally following question: If God intends to deal equitably with men, why does He let all men die unvindicated or unpunished? It is designed by God, the Preacher says, to put men to a winnowing test, to reveal their hearts. Justice delayed will embolden the wicked to further evil (8.11) but it will humble the righteous and move them to greater trust in God (Deut 8.2–3). One can only imagine the hypocrisy in a world where evil was immediately punished and good immediately rewarded.

# Men Like Beasts

*"I said in my heart, 'Concerning the condition of the sons of men, God tests them, that they may see that they them selves are like animals'. For what happens to the sons of men also happens to animals; one things befalls them: as one dies, so dies the other. Surely, they have no advantage over animals, for all is vanity. All go to one place: all are from the dust, and all will return to dust. Who knows the spirit of the sons of men, which goes upward, and the spirit of the animal, which goes down to the earth?" (Ecc 3.18–21).*

This section of Ecclesiastes is not an easy one to sort out but it is terribly mistaken to see in it an expression of Solomon's cynicism, the words of a man hopelessly distressed by life's injustice and brevity. If so he must be seriously conflicted. How are we to reconcile such a view with the Preacher's regularly expressed confidence that however jarringly contradictory things on earth may appear God has so arranged them that "in His time" they will issue in a result both graciously wonderful (3.11) and just (3.17)? These themes can be brought together by recognizing that Solomon is dealing candidly with life as seen from beneath the sun, and then reaching above the sun for the confidence that these now baffling circumstances will not be left as they are. His point throughout the book seems to be that although the work of God in human affairs often mystifies us, He is working nonetheless (3.11; 8.17) and working with justice and grace.

Solomon's point is well taken. The fact that we know so little of God's providential working from our present vantage point should not only keep us humble but restrain us from hasty explanations of life's heart-breaking tragedies. There are things we must be content not to know or understand (Deut 29.29). Comfort and assurance will have to come from simply knowing and trusting God (2 Tim 3.12b). Though Eliphaz's presumption of Job's guilt was wrong, his counsel for life's painful perplexities is right. "But as for me, I would seek God, and to God I would commit my cause—who does great things, and unsearchable ..." (Job 5.8–9).

In former verses Solomon has wrestled with death's blindness to whether a man is wise or foolish (2.14–16). All come to the same end, he will later say, whether they are rich or poor (6.6), righteous or wicked (9.2). This fact of life, left unresolved, would make life meaningless and without purpose. Now Solomon presses the point that not only is there no distinction between men in death but there is no distinction between men and animals (3.19–21). Yet his purpose now is not to raise a problem but to solve one. Why are all men taken down to the dust? Justice, he says, may not exist under the sun, but God will at last judge all men (3.16–17). And because that is true, death not only cannot frustrate God's righteous judgment but God uses it to help men see that they are not gods, all-powerful and self-sufficient, but at least in one respect just like the animals. Made of dust, they return to dust (Gen 2.7; 3.19). Death, as a gracious warning, is intended to open the hearts of men to their true nature as creatures and draw them out of their sinful rebellion and back to God (Rom 8.20).

The words of Solomon are not unique. One psalmist virtually repeats them. "Nevertheless man, though in honor, does not remain; he is like the beasts that perish … like sheep they are laid in the grave …" (Psa 49.12, 14).The point is that our physical frailty demonstrates that we are not masters of our own lot in life however in our arrogant foolishness we imagine it otherwise.

There is no question that we share with animals the same physical life force which is destined for the grave and that in so far as the life of the flesh is concerned we have no advantage over beasts. And if it is true that Solomon is saying in verse 21 that we don't know that the ultimate destiny of man differs from the beasts (disputed by Leupold and in the translation of the NKJV. James E. Smith sees it as saying the very opposite and a corrective of potential misinterpretation of preceding statements, *Wisdom, Literature and Psalms*, p. 735), he is speaking in terms of human knowledge and our limited point of observation beneath the sun. For there is no question that the Preacher understands the imperishable nature and special destiny of men (8.12–13; 12.7).

Finally, Solomon concludes by repeating what he has already said (v 12), that man, vulnerable to grave injustices and powerless before the forces of nature, should trust God to make all things right at last and live joyfully in His present gifts (v 22).

# The Search for Justice and Contentment: *Ecclesiastes 4.1–6*

*Then I returned and considered all the oppression that is done under the sun: And look! The tears of the oppressed, but they have no comforter—On the side of their oppressors there is power, but they have no comforter.*

*Therefore I praised the dead who were already dead, more than the living who are still alive. Yet, better than both is he who has never existed, who has not seen the evil work that is done under the sun" (Ecc 4.1–3)*

## The Innocent Mercilessly Oppressed

As this chapter opens Solomon revisits his earlier observation about wickedness in the courts (3.16) with a moving description of the misery this injustice in high places inflicts on the innocent. Thoughts of their tearful pleadings before the crushing power of merciless oppressors who have driven off all their comforters filled the Preacher with despair and indignation. Were there nothing more than earth's "justice," surely oppressed people would be better off dead or, still better, never born. In his despair over a hellish oppression which seemed to be winning, Elijah once prayed to die (1 Kgs 19.4); and the merciless injustices visited on Jeremiah made him wish for a moment that he had never been born (Jer 20.14–18). Justice, the Preacher accurately observes, is difficult to find under the sun while brutal oppression is not. As Paul, in speaking of the resurrection, once concluded, "If in this life only we have hope in Christ, we are of all men the most pitiable" (1 Cor 15.19). If what we see on earth is all there is we would surely be better off dead or unborn. But that is not all there is and the apparent despair of the Preacher's words here must be balanced with those already written (3.17) and soon to be written: "Though a sinner does evil a hundred times, and his days are prolonged, yet I surely know that it will be well with those who fear God, who fear before Him. But it will not be well with the wicked; nor will he prolong his days, which are as a shadow, because he does not fear before God" (8.12–13). The counsel of the psalmist is true: "It is better to trust in the Lord than to put confidence in man. It is better to trust in the Lord than to put confidence in princes" (Psa 118.8–9).

## The Emptiness of Mindless Work

"Again, I saw that for all toil and every skillful work a man is envied by his neighbor. This also is vanity and a grasping for the wind" (4.4).

If it is a grave mistake to build your life on the thought that there will always be justice in this life, it is an equally grave error to presume that you can work your way to happiness. Work and what it can achieve is severely limited. Instead of admiration and appreciation for what one has gained from his labor Solomon warns that the race to achieve will lead only to an envy driven strife in a dog-eat-dog world. It is a world in which there are no "neighbors," only rivals.

The secret does not lie in indolence (4.5) but in a contentment borne of a realization of the limitations of work as well as its value. "Better is a handful with quietness than both hands full, together with toil and grasping for the wind." (4.6). Ray Pritchard tells the story of a conversation between a hard-driving corporate attorney and a professional fisherman friend whom he found teaching his two young sons to catch crabs. "Why aren't you out fishing," he asked. "Because I've caught enough fish for today," his friend replied. "But why don't you catch more fish than you need?" "What would I do with them?" responded the fisherman. "You could earn more money and buy a better boat so you could catch more fish. Then you could buy a fleet of boats and soon be rich like me." "What would I do then?" "You could sit down and enjoy life." "What do you think I'm doing now?" the fisherman replied. Simply put, a job is not the meaning of life nor what it earns you a measure of your worth. There are far more important things that all that industry cannot buy. Immensely more important is how all our activity serves to produce a godly character and to build a solid relationship with God and others.

This same wisdom is reflected in Solomon's proverbs: "Better is a little with the fear of the Lord, than great treasure with trouble. Better is a dinner of herbs where love is, than a fatted calf with hatred" (Prov 15.16–17. cf. 16.8). Paul echoes it in 1 Timothy: "Now godliness with contentment is great gain. For we brought nothing into this world, and it is certain we can carry nothing out. And having food and clothing, with these we shall be content" (6.6–8).

This is so patently true but how seldom understood and practiced, even by Christians!

# People are More Important than Things: *Ecclesiastes 4.7–16*

*"Then I returned, and I saw vanity under the sun: There is one alone, without companion: He has neither son nor brother. Yet there is no end to all his labors, nor is his eye satisfied with riches. But he never asks, 'for whom do I toil and deprive myself of good?' This also is vanity and a grave misfortune" (4.7–8).*

It is a tragic truth that many people put their heads down and plow through life without ever asking what life is all about or whether what they are doing makes any lasting sense. Such is the case that Solomon describes. This man is a mindless workaholic who grinds on day after day piling his treasures higher and higher. And yet he finds no fulfillment in either his achievements or their product. He cannot even say that he is doing it for his family as many such deluded individuals claim; and if he had possessed a family his obsessive behavior would have long since alienated them. The chances are that he was as devoid of friends as he was of family. Such people only have confederates who are equally fixated. Solomon's high achiever was destined not only to be empty but also to be exquisitely lonely. It is indeed a "grave misfortune" when we live our lives thinking that pride-driven achievement and material success are more important than people.

We need to tell ourselves the truth about mere things. The immensely wealthy high-achieving Solomon spoke it: "He who loves silver will not be satisfied with silver; nor he that loves abundance with increase. This also is vanity" (5.10).

There is no one who owns more than God (Psa 50.12) but divine joy is found not in creating and possessing "all things wise and wonderful" but in sharing them. God's great labor in creation and His eternal purpose in His Son were focused not on Himself but on sharing His glory with men (Heb 2.10). He is the great servant God who delightedly empties out the treasures of His power and love upon others. We need to be equally wise.

## The Value of a Friend

*"Two are better than one, because they have a good reward for their labor. For if one fall, one will lift up his companion. But woe to him who is alone when he falls, for he has no one to help him up"* (4.9–10).

In verses 9–12 the Preacher stresses our weakness and vulnerability as human beings and the importance of others in our lives. It may be a delight to the ego to say that we don't need anybody but it is a lie. All we have ever done since we were born was to need somebody—somebody to carry us about, feed us and dress us, someone to provide for us, protect us, teach us, love us, befriend us, encourage us, and share life with us. And overarching all the human help we have needed is the sustaining grace of a God who "gives to all life and breath and all things" (Acts 17.25). It is that very God who said in the beginning that "it is not good that man should be alone" (Gen 2.18).

More than that, in the broadest sense, it is not possible. We are by nature dependent creatures.

The Preacher's message is that we need friends and companions to pick us up when we fall, to warm us when life grows hard and cold, to encourage and uphold us when we are under assault, or just to enlarge life's joys by giving us someone to share them with.

Some fear the hurt that getting close to others may bring but that is nothing compared to the agony of isolation. Aloneness is awful. Love is always a risk. Ask God. But it is a risk well worth the taking. Naomi needs her Ruth. Moses his Joshua. David his Jonathan. Paul his Timothy.

## Popularity is Fickle

*"Better a poor and wise youth than an old and foolish king who will be admonished no more. For he comes out of prison to be king, although he was born poor in his kingdom. I saw all the living who walk under the sun; they were with the second youth who stands in his place. There was no end of all the people over whom he was made king. Yet those who come afterward will not rejoice in him. Surely this also is vanity and grasping for the wind"* (4.13–16).

It is one thing to live trustingly with friends, it is quite another to be seduced by shallow "popularity." Here Solomon concludes his "better" observations (4.3, 6, 9, 13). An old king grown foolish with pride and self-conceit and considering himself irreplaceable may soon be removed by a poor but wise youth who arises from, of all places, a prison cell. Proud Irreplaceable is often turned out by Humble and Wise Unlikely (Preachers take note). But be warned. Young men with wisdom and skill can often have their own heads turned by the popularity that sweeps them up and can just as decisively sweep them out. This, too, is vanity. Only God is ultimately trustworthy.

# God Amid the Shadows
## *Ecclesiastes 5.1–7*

Solomon has so far made very clear that his search for ultimate meaning in the world "beneath the sun" has been fruitless. The endless cycle of nature appears to be going nowhere, producing nothing new. Both eye and ear are left unsatisfied (1.3–8). Wisdom, pleasure, wealth and great enterprises, however useful for the moment, not only leave the soul unfulfilled but end in death (1.12–2.26; 3.19–21). They are but "grasping for the wind".

The world is filled with the mystery of jarring contradictions which are beyond man's control and defy human understanding however much one strives to make sense of them (3.1–11). Indeed, God has so made men that they are driven by nature to seek transcendent meaning for their lives. He has "put eternity in their hearts." Yet for all their wisdom, wealth and power (and Solomon had plenty of each) they are unable to penetrate the mystery and discover life's ultimate meaning and purpose here (3.11).

Solomon is also challenged by the rampant injustice and oppression that inhabited the world he knew. Where justice should have been found there was wickedness (3.16). The poor and defenseless instead of being protected were made the prey of the powerful. Their cries for relief were unheard. And if this is the final end of things, Solomon observes that it was better they had never been born (4.1–3).

These incontrovertible realities made belief in a just and omnipotent God difficult but not impossible. Solomon even as he raises these difficulties in the visible world rather regularly reaches up to God. He is convinced that God "has made everything beautiful in its time" (3.11), a foreshadowing of Paul's confident affirmation, "And we know that all things work together for good to those who love God, to those who are the called according to His purpose" (Rom. 8.28). For the Preacher all these shattering puzzles which he has raised will be worked by a wise and loving God into a fabric of eternal beauty.

And as for the undeniable grave injustices worked under the sun he is confident that "God shall judge the righteous and the wicked, for there is a time there for every purpose and for every work" (3.17). Everything at last, beyond this world, will be brought to equity. This theme continues throughout the book. This Preacher is no cynic.

Ecclesiastes 5.1–7 almost seems to be an interlude as it rises without apparent context. A possible solution is Solomon's anticipation of an indifferent approach to God because of all life's apparent contradictions which seem to bring His power and righteousness into doubt. That is the view of one student of the book when he writes, "Obstacles there are to believing in God's omnipotence, but none of them should be used as an excuse for neglecting one's relationship to God who said He is actively in charge of all things" (Walter C. Kaiser, Jr., *Ecclesiastes: Total Life, p. 74*). There is an incident in the interaction between Christ and His disciples that answers the question of what should be done when we do not understand what God is doing. In John 6 Jesus has refused to be the king of bread to some of His carnal disciples much impressed by the feeding of the 5,000. When they seek Him looking for more fish and bread He identifies *Himself* as the bread of life, upon which many of His disciples walked away. Jesus then turns to His remaining but still uncomprehending disciples and asks, "Do you also want to go away?" To which Peter replies most wisely, "Lord, to whom shall we go? You have the words of eternal life. Also we have come to believe and know that You are the Christ, the Son of the living God" (John 6.67–69).

Some might observe that we are no longer in Solomon's position of limited revelation before Jesus and the New Testament. That may be true but we are still confronted by the same puzzling apparent contradictions with which Solomon wrestled. And no explanations are given. That is why Deuteronomy 29.29 is still comforting. Like Job, even when we do not understand why things are happening as they are, and God is not disposed to explain, we must trust Him, knowing that we in our very limited knowledge are in no position to judge Him who possesses both infinite knowledge and power (Job 42.1–6). And since Jesus has died how can we question God's love?

James Russell Lowell spoke poetically to this question many years ago.

> Though the cause of evil prosper,
> Yet 'tis truth alone is strong.
> Truth forever on the scaffold
> Wrong forever on the throne
> Yet that scaffold sways the future
> And behind the dim unknown
> Standeth God amid the shadows
> Keeping watch above His own.

It is not the throne of evil that ultimately succeeds. It is the cross, the place of apparent despair and defeat, the place of poverty and emptiness and nothingness.

We pray, Father, that You will take the scales from our eyes that we might see life as You see it, that we might look at events of our day, not from the puny viewpoint of the flesh, but rather from the viewpoint of these great eternal visions which allow us to see things as they really are. (Ray Stedman)

# Words, Words, Words
# Promises, Promises!

*"Walk prudently when you go to the house of God; and draw near to hear rather than to offer the sacrifice of fools, for they do not know that they do evil. Do not be rash with your mouth, and let not your heart utter anything hastily before God. For God is in heaven and you on earth; therefore let your words be few" (Ecc 5.1–2).*

Here the language of reflection in 4.1–16 changes to the language of instruction in 5.1–7. Addressing his readers for the first time with the second personal "you" the Preacher seems to be saying, "This is important. Pay attention". This section begins and ends with admonitions concerning our attitude toward God. But this is not Solomon's first word on this subject. Indeed he has said that the reason God has ordered the world as it is (3.1–11) is so "that men should fear before Him" (3.14b). This will surface again in the book (7.18; 8.12–13) and at last be the concluding charge (12.13). As has been quite accurately observed, "What comes into our minds when we think about God is the most important thing about us." Our attitude toward God determines our attitude toward everything else.

The fifth chapter opens with a sobering warning about our approach to God. It is couched in language meaningful for the times when "the house of God" referred to the temple, the place toward which the prayers of Israel were to be directed (1 Kgs 8.29–30; Jon 2.4; Dan 6.10). That approach, says the Preacher, was to be made with utmost sobriety and care.

The core problem of our failure to deal with God as we ought is too small a grasp of or even an inaccurate view of who He is. He is surely merciful and gracious (Exod 33.6) but He is also above and beyond all that we might imagine in wisdom, power and righteousness (Isa 40.25–26; Psa 119.142). There is therefore utmost danger in toying with such a God (Deut 4.24; Luke 12.5; Heb 10.31; 12.28–29). As Solomon says, "For God is in heaven and you are on the earth" (5.2). It is He, not you, who rules. His knowledge is limitless, yours tiny by comparison.

We should therefore approach Him in awe struck wonder that the eternally righteous God would allow the likes of us to draw near to Him (Isa 6.5; Luke 5.8). And we should also move into His presence with silence, a silence born of a submissive willingness to listen rather than to talk. We must "draw near to hear" the One whose knowledge and wisdom are infinite. We are hardly in a position to instruct Him (Job 21.22; Isa 40.12–15; Rom 11.33–34). And the Hebrew verb translated "hear" in this text means "to hear so as to do". So, before we open our mouths to God let us take time to reverently consider who we are dealing with. The sobering counsel of Habakkuk is appropriate: "But the Lord is in His holy temple. Let all the earth keep silence before Him" (2.20). Especially when dealing with God it is imperative to think carefully before you speak.

The right approach to God will deliver us from offering "the sacrifice of fools" which the Preacher says is "evil". But the fool, amazingly enough, does not know it! Perhaps it is because he has been talking instead of listening. There is clear indication in this warning that attitude takes priority even over act in the worship of God. David understood this when in his penitential psalm he says that mere sacrifices cannot substitute for "a broken spirit and a contrite heart" (Psa 51.16–17). Isaiah says that sacrifices from ungodly people are repugnant to God (1.10–15). So also Amos (5.21–24), Micah (6.6–8) and Hosea: "For I desire mercy and not sacrifice, and the knowledge of God more than burnt offerings" (6.6). So it is the fool who imagines he can robotically follow the outward forms of divinely prescribed worship and treat with contempt God's moral and spiritual will. But he is no less a fool who imagines that as long as his intention is worshipful, the form God has prescribed for that worship need not concern him. Aaron's two elder sons and Saul the king would strongly disagree (Lev 10.1–3; 1 Sam 15.16–23). Actually, we cannot be worshiping God when our own will takes precedence over His (John 6.38).

We need therefore to measure our words when we come into the presence of the Almighty. Mindless babble which has no depth of heart or thought will not do. Perhaps the proverbial admonition of James would especially apply to our interactions with God: "So then, my beloved brethren, let every man be swift to hear, slow to speak" (1.19).

### "When you make a vow to God do not delay to pay it... ."

After telling us to watch what we say in the presence of God, the Preacher tells us to do what we say. Vows of OT devotions were usually made in the context of public worship (Psa 50.14; 76.11). They were voluntary, not required, and when made were to be kept. Human beings are prone to rattling off heedless promises which make us feel better at the moment but are quickly forgotten. That is hardly commendable when it involves others but is tragic when it involves God. All who are Christians make a vow to follow Jesus as Lord. All who marry make a vow to each other and to God to be faithful to the marriage covenant. Such vows are solemn and are to be kept. No excuses will be accepted. The promises we make to God in spiritual songs are often made mindlessly but God will take them seriously. It was A. W. Tozer who said that Christians never lie unless they are singing. Koheleth counsels us not to make vows if we do not intend to keep them. Don't try to play games with God.

# When Wealth Becomes Toxic: *Ecclesiastes 5.8–20*

The wisdom literature has much to say about wealth and may at times seem contradictory. To some extent this is true of Eccle-siastes which, while speaking of the transcendent emptiness of material riches, can still commend their value (7.12; 11.19). Nei-ther Proverbs nor Ecclesiastes is saying that wealth has no value, but that it has no essential or eternal value. The same is true of practical wisdom. Solomon does not say that such wisdom (of which he had a lot) has no value, but that it has no ultimate value. This difference in perspective is necessary if we are to properly understand Ecclesiastes.

In these verses, as well as the first 9 verses of chapter 6, Solo-mon warns of the great dangers resident in material wealth. First of all, he says that we should not be shocked at the chain of op-pression which afflicts a world in which things are more import-ant than people. The poor take a hard hit because they are op-pressed by everybody. The Preacher describes the systemic social corruption in which the rich and powerful support each other in the stripping of the unfortunate and rulers serve themselves, heedless of the needs of those they rule. This injustice has earlier deeply distressed him (4.1; cf. Job 35.9). Some may object that this was hardly the case in the kingdom of Solomon. Not indeed at its beginning but certainly towards its end (1 Kgs 12.2–4). Yet that is not Solomon's focus. His perspective is not merely the world of Israel, but that of all men, a world where money is treasured and people used.

In verse 9, although the Hebrew text is "both terse and cryptic" (David Hubbard, *Ecclesiastes, Song of Solomon,* p. 137), Solomon seems to speak of a more equitable situation in which the tilled land benefits all, both laborers and owners, both ruled and ruler.

In verse 10 and following, Koheleth traces the sorrows which come from the deification of riches. Material wealth is a treacherous god. It does not provide what it promises. It cannot bring fulfillment to the human spirit. "He who loves silver will not be satisfied with silver, nor he who loves abundance with increase" (5.10). The thirst for things is unquenchable. The extremely wealthy John D. Rockefeller expressed it when asked how much money it took to satisfy a man. "Just a little more," he replied. Schopenhauer describes it as being like drinking seawater. The more you drink the thirstier you get. Covetousness brings no peace (6.7–9). Indeed the whole world could not fill the emptiness inside a single human heart (Matt 16.26). Solomon surely knew this well. It was "grasping for the wind." The problem, of course, is not money, but the love of it (1 Tim 6.9–10) and the trust in it (1 Tim 6.17). It is that state in which what we have becomes who we are (Luke 12.15) and what we possess comes to possess us.

Secondly, wealth attracts an increasing number of dependents, hangers-on who are drawn like bees to the honey (5.11). Expenses rise to meet income. The more one has, the more it takes to maintain it.

Thirdly, material prosperity not only does not bring peace, but can destroy it. The poor laboring man leads a simple life and sleeps soundly in his weariness while the rich man cannot sleep for worry over holding onto and increasing what he has (5.12). That is what happens when what you have is who you are.

Fourthly, riches can vanish as quickly as they come (5.13–14; 6.1–2). "Will you set your eyes on that which is not? For riches certainly make for themselves wings; they fly away like an eagle toward heaven" (Prov 23.5). Circumstances beyond our control are at work in this world and for all our prudence, wealth can be snatched away. For the one whose treasures are earthly, there is no tragedy so severe as their loss. They have lost themselves.

And finally, there is that most obvious and sobering reality about physical wealth. Even if one manages to retain his riches throughout his lifetime, death at last will strip it all away (5.15–17). Here Solomon echoes Job (1.21) and repeats the conclusion of his own futile search for ultimate meaning beneath the sun (Ecc 2.15–23). Both wise and foolish, rich and poor, great and small, all die and leave everything behind. They will leave in the same nakedness in which they came.

Still, Solomon does not leave this contemplation of the tragedy of a life lived for things in despair of the usefulness of life's material gifts. He says here as he does frequently in Ecclesiastes that even though these things have only a temporal use, they should be received with gratitude and enjoyed as "the gift of God" (5.18–20; note also 2.24; 3.12–13; 8.15; 9.7–9). In other words, take them as God grants them to you, but do not make them what life is all about. That's what makes them toxic.

# Living a Meaningful Life in a Meaningless World: *Ecclesiastes 6.1–12*

The Preacher has shown that enjoyment as a gift from God is far preferable to accumulating many possessions or attempting to be wise enough to explain every mystery and master every eventuality (which he says is "chasing the wind"). The satisfaction and enjoyment of which he speaks in 5.18–20 is not in the abundance of things or the lack of them which one receives but in accepting it gratefully and trustingly as the lot which God has granted. Keil and Delitzsch put it this way: "Cheerful enjoyment is in this life that which is most advisable; but also it is not made possible in itself by the possession of earthly treasures—it is yet a special gift of God added thereto." (Old Testament Commentaries, Vol. 4, p. 1026)

In chapter six Solomon returns to his warnings about the emptiness of wealth when seen as life's meaning and purpose. He has already pressed home three brutal facts about wealth: 1) It will never satisfy the human spirit (5.10) and, even if it could 2) it is fleeting and uncertain (5.13–14); and at last death will inevitably steal it all away (5.16–17). Now, having spoken of one to whom God has granted both wealth and the ability to enjoy it, the Preacher introduces an opposing "evil" (misfortune). And God is involved in this, too. God gives a man riches in such abundance as to fulfill all his desires, but then deprives him of the ability to enjoy it. That privilege falls to others, to strangers rather than his own children. No explanation is given for the man's grievous loss. Perhaps he squandered the opportunity to enjoy it while he had it because he was busy trying to get more. Or perhaps it was due to no fault of his own. Time and chance happen to all (9.11).

Why does God let such things happen? God's providence is often quite impenetrable for those of us "under the sun". Do they actually occur? Yes. Job comes quickly to mind. He was a righteous man and rich yet God allowed him to lose all his wealth, his children and his health. It was an agonizing experience for Job and God never explained to him the reason why. His wealth and health were restored but only after he had learned to trust God whatever his material situation. Perhaps at times such "grievous evils" are a painful reminder that from God's perspective none of those things are the measure of a life enjoyed and well-lived. As Jesus' parable of the Rich Farmer reminds us it is a dangerous thing to put your confidence in riches (Luke 12.13–21).

But what if the one in question did not lose his wealth (6.3–6)? What if he had a hundred children and lived many years, even two thousand! They would mean nothing if he never learned to enjoy them day to day as a gift of God and look beyond them to the greater riches. No matter how full and how long his life death will ultimately take it all away and his wasted life will make a stillborn child better off than he. It can never miss what it never knew.

In verses 7–9 Solomon sums up his observations about the emptiness of chasing material things. "All the labor of man is for his mouth," he says, " and yet his soul is not satisfied." In our pursuit of the things that feed the physical man we must remember that we are far more than that. Above all the spirit must be fed for as Moses said to Israel, and Jesus repeated to Satan, "Man shall not live by bread alone but by every word that proceeds from the mouth of God" (Deut 8.3; Matt 4.4). Therefore, in the final analysis the secret of the joyful life does not lie in whether as regards this world you are rich or poor, shrewd or inept. Better, he says, than the "wandering of the appetite (ESV)," the endless seeking for more, is contentment with what one has (i.e. what the eye can see). Anything else he repeats again is just "grasping for the wind."

In verses 10–12 the Preacher addresses the hopelessness of fighting against divine providence. We may struggle against the nature of this broken world beneath the sun which God has purposely brought to vanity (Rom 8.20) but it is a hopeless struggle as all the past proclaims. Mere man cannot contend with God (ill. Job). It is an exercise in futility. God alone knows and holds the future and He alone "knows what is good for man in life". Our task, as cannot be missed in this great book, is simply to trust Him and do His will.

# Making Wise Choices in an Uncertain World: *Ecclesiastes 7.1–4*

Solomon appears in chapter 7 to be responding to the questions he raised in 6.12. He now strings together a series of proverbs which address wise ways to choose in a world of great uncertainty. These "better than" comparisons contrast what may be pleasant with what is wise, what is momentarily appealing with what is lastingly valuable. Or as one writer has put it, "There are times when bad is better." Some of the medicines that taste the worst may produce the best cure. In this case Solomon seems to be saying again that adversity is better than prosperity.

The Preacher begins by declaring that "a good name" (reflective of one's character) is far more significant than "precious ointment" (a good smell). The first has depth and lasting meaning; the last only a passing pleasant odor which says nothing meaningful about the one who wears it. It is all so superficial and momentary. The most precious of perfumes cannot cover the stink of a bad character. Solomon is not inveighing here against the use of ointments. They served some useful purposes in the New Testament. They were instruments of kindness to guests (Luke 7.45–46; John 12.3), a means of caring for the dead (John 19.39–40). But they pale in significance to what we truly are within. It is also possible that the "precious ointment" is indicative of wealth. Solomon had

in an earlier proverb made this point: "A good name is to be chosen rather than great riches, Loving favor rather than silver and
gold." (Prov 22.1). Wealth, too, is superficial and passing.

Solomon's next proverb is a bit of a stunner: "And the day
of death than the day of one's birth." How can birth, a time of
great rejoicing, be compared unfavorably to death, a time of
great sadness? Perhaps it must be understood in context. For
the man who has chosen a good name, a godly character, over
mere things, death is the end of a race well run; akin to Paul's
valedictory written to Timothy: I have fought the good fight, I
have finished the course, I have kept the faith. (2 Tim 4.7). There
are two occasions when our name is specially significant, at birth
and in our obituary. So these two dates are inscribed with a dash
between them on many a tomb stone. Birth is filled with promise
but it is what happens between those two dates that has lasting
consequences and significance. The time does fly by but it is sufficient to become God's servant or to commit great foolishness.

The Preacher turns immediately to consider where the truly
wise will find themselves in the midst of life's conflicting circumstances. It is better, he says, to go to "the house of mourning" (a
funeral) than to "the house of feasting". Times of pleasure are
not forbidden by Solomon (2.24; 8.15; 9.7–9). They simply do not
teach life's vital lessons. Funerals remind us of the unpleasant but
critical truth that all of us die. The wise will face squarely the
fragility and temporariness of life in the flesh and order their lives
accordingly. Whatever we may suppose pain and sorrow are a far
better teacher than pleasure.

Thomas Gray's Elegy Written in a Country Church Yard
speaks powerfully of our common destiny:

> The boast of heraldry, the pomp of power,
> All that beauty, and all that wealth e›er gave

Awaits alike the inevitable hour.
The paths of glory lead but to the grave.

Two Old Testament worthies urge us most earnestly to contemplate the brevity and fragile nature of our lives. Moses, speaking plainly of life's brevity, entreats God: "So teach us to number our days, that we may gain a heart of wisdom." (Psa 90.12). David, too, appeals in Psalm 39.4: "LORD, make me to know my end, and what is the measure of my days, that I may know how frail I am."

Solomon concludes this segment of his proverbs by saying that, "Sorrow is better than laughter for by a sad countenance the heart is made better." (7.3). Here the Preacher stretches a point to make one. Sorrow is not always better than laughter for he once said as much (Prov 15.13; 17.22), but in this context when it is either sober thought or endless party hopping it is a far better choice. Here he emphasizes the point already made that bad times have a far greater impact on our hearts than times of ease. Even our Lord learned through suffering (Heb 5.8).

So, as he concludes, "The heart of the wise is in the house of mourning (Matt 5.3), but the heart of fools is in the house of mirth" (7.4).

Robert Frost, the New England Poet, wrote: "Two roads converged in a wood, and I—I took the one less traveled by and that has made all the difference." Solomon has placed us at the fork in the road. We are advised to take the road of divine wisdom which will always be the road less traveled.

# Faithful Are the Wounds of a Friend: *Ecclesiastes 7.5–10*

Solomon began this chapter with the clear assertion that wisdom grows out of squarely facing life's brevity and death's inevitability. Sorrow, he says, is a far better teacher than laughter. Now, from the implicit admonition that comes from spending time in the presence of death, Solomon turns to the importance of accepting the explicit reproof of the wise. The Preacher recognizes as he gives this counsel that being corrected is painful to the ego and our first impulse will be to reject it. The book of Proverbs is full of warnings on this subject. "The way of a fool is right in his own eyes, but he who heeds counsel is wise" (12.15; cf. 14.12; 16.2, 25; and 21.2).

The willingness to receive counsel and correction from wiser heads is critical. The wise in this admonition are clearly those who are wise in the ways of God and who have our best interest at heart and not their own. It is far more pleasant to listen to the mindless approval of fools, but to be seduced by their fawning complements is hazardous. It is a dangerous time when everyone is singing our praises (Luke 6.26). Solomon has been on this subject before. "Faithful are the wounds of a friend, but the kisses of an enemy are deceitful" (Prov 27.6). So we need to cherish the friends who care enough for us to correct us even at the risk of the relationship. Nathan's rebuke of David was truly a risky business.

David was the king and had already arranged the death of one good man who got in his way. But Nathan loved David and gave him what he desperately needed, a good dose of the truth.

We all need the courage and good sense to accept correction, however painful. It is surely ill grace in those who correct others by preaching and teaching to summarily reject any effort to correct themselves. "You, therefore, who teach others, do you not teach yourself?" (Rom 2.21). But, the rejoinder comes, "Their criticisms are bad-spirited." Perhaps, but can we not learn even from the rebuke of our enemies? If they are correct, are we not benefited, regardless of motive? A gospel preacher friend once told me of an occasion when some brother in Christ called him a liar. He went for counsel to an older preacher whose first response to his complaint was, "Well, are you?" Whenever accused, should that not be our first question?

We cannot with wisdom spend all our lives in "the house of mirth" where shallow and sometimes unholy laughter acts as a sedative to dull our emptiness. As Solomon says, the song of fools is like burning thorns under a pot (nettles under a kettle) which leap up in a flash of flame, but bring no lasting benefit. When we are captivated by the apparent glory of this passing world we are doomed to miss the critical and lasting lessons that come from divine wisdom. It is not advisable to go whistling through the graveyard. We are well advised by the Preacher not to be extorted or bribed into stupidity by the pressures or temptations of this present age (7.7). We must be wise enough to look down the different paths before us and determine where they are leading. It is not how we begin, but how we end that matters. We must not be discouraged by the difficulties of the right path or spend our time railing angrily against life's unfairness and injustice. Trust in God's gracious providence and the patient pursuit of His wise way and its far better end is what is needed. Anger and impatience are found in the heart of a fool (7.8–9). It is not the circumstances of life under the sun that determine the wisdom of our course, but what God will judge it to be at journey's end.

The tenth verse has been a challenge to students of Ecclesiastes, but remembering that Ecclesiastes is not like Proverbs, a series at times of discrete wise sayings that do not necessarily have any connection with each other. The Preacher has a purpose and presses important themes. They may spiral sometimes repetitively through the book but yet have context. "Do not say," he cautions, "'Why are the former days better than these?' For you do not inquire wisely concerning this." Is this not a warning about living in the past and cursing the present. A constant lament about the world going to the dogs will not help us to live wisely in the world as it is. It is an attitude filled with pessimism and despair, and inaction. The world has always been "going to the dogs," but God's in His heaven and we can serve Him no matter what.

# Who Can Make Straight What God Has Made Crooked? *Ecclesiastes 7.11–15*

Following in the wake of several proverbs which speak of the advantage of sorrow, Solomon pauses again to praise wisdom and understanding as a blessing to those under the sun. Prudence serves, he says, to protect its possessor, even as inherited money may (when it does not become the object of life) but wisdom exceeds money in value because it preserves life while money in the hands of a fool can bring disaster (7.11–12). At last, as Solomon has said repeatedly in Proverbs, "the beginning of wisdom is the fear of the Lord, and the knowledge of the Holy One is understanding" (Prov 9.10). Our wisdom cannot penetrate nor rationalize all of God's providential ways (3:14b; 6.12; 8.16–17) so the fear of the Lord (reverential trust and submission) must be the anchor that guides us through all of life's exigencies (5.7; 7.18; 12.13) and the Preacher has listed a multitude of them. Wickedness and iniquity rather than righteousness (3.15). The merciless oppression of the powerless (4.1). The swift and sudden loss of all things material (5.13–15). The puzzling providence that allows a just man to perish in his righteousness and a wicked man to prolong his life in wickedness (7.15; 8.14). Things here are not just filled with adversity, they are often morally and ethically misaligned. The challenge is that all this adversity and inequity under the sun happen either by God's design or permission for He has appointed both the day of prosperity and the day of adversity and one cannot anticipate which will come (7.14).

In the very beginning of his book Solomon described very decisively the nature of life under the sun: "What is crooked," he said, "cannot be made straight, and what is lacking cannot be numbered" (1.15). Now he calls upon his readers to consider this condition as "the work of God" (7.13). And that is the reason that no human effort can straighten what is bent and supply what is lacking. We don't live today in the perfect world of Genesis 1 and 2 but in the crooked and flawed world of Genesis 3 which God intentionally "subjected to vanity" (Rom 8.20). Suffering and death entered where perfection and peace had once reigned. Jarring contradictions now plague human life (3.1–8), and yet God did even this graciously "in hope" (Rom 8.20b) so that men should learn to submit to and wait on Him in utter trust (3.14b). Solomon is correct in saying that the world in which we live is one in which "The race is not to the swift, nor the battle to the strong, nor bread to the wise, nor riches to men of understanding, nor favor to men of skill; but time and chance happen to them all" (Ecc 9.11).

The Bible is filled with ethical puzzles. We are told, of course, why Jesus had to die, but why did Abel have to die, certainly childless and likely unmarried, while his murderer lived on? Why did righteous Job have to suffer so profoundly? Why did some of God's Old Testament prophets have to endure such abuse from ungodly rulers and live such hounded lives? And in the New Testament. Why did John the Baptist, the herald of the Messiah and His kingdom, suffer execution without ever knowing family life and children? Why did Stephen have to be stoned to death while Philip lived to marry and preach many years? Why was the apostle James executed and his brother John allowed to live to a ripe old age? We really do not know with any certainty the answer to these questions but we must rest easy with the knowledge that though we do not know what God is doing, He does. He is working all things according to the counsel of His will, and His will toward us is gracious (Jer 29.11; Rom 5.6–11; 8.28). Things will not be worked out in equity and justice in the short term. God's loving purpose for us will not be fulfilled in the world beneath the sun. But beyond this universe of time and space, it will be. It absolutely will be. If we will only wait patiently for it (Psa 27; Psa 130; Isa 30.18; 40.31; Lam 3.22–26; Phil 3.20–21).

So how are we to react to life's frequently jarring contradictions and uncertainties? Solomon says that in prosperous times we should rejoice and thank God who gave them (not, however, resting our hope on their continuance); and in times of adversity we are to "consider." We should consider that God's love for us is not determined by our physical and material circumstances (Rom 8.35–39). His love for the rich and the poor is equivalent (Prov 22.2). Remember Lazarus in Jesus' story? And it will remind us how totally dependent we are on God for everything (Acts 17.28) and stir us to the profoundest gratitude and praise.

# Attempting to Game Divine Providence

Solomon has made clear from the book's beginning that human wisdom, though practically valuable (6.11–12), is not only incapable of providing ultimate answers but cannot predict the future or determine outcomes in this life (1.16–18; 3.11, 14; 7.15; 8.14). The world beneath the sun, broken and cursed by the divine will (Gen 3; Rom 8.20), cannot be mastered and rationalized by human powers. God's providence cannot be fully known through human efforts however determined they may be (8.17). This is one of the Preacher's axioms.

It is in this context that Ecclesiastes 7.16–18 may be properly understood. These verses, so startling on the surface, are not easily deciphered. They have challenged many a student of the book. But one understanding should be excluded from the outset. Solomon is certainly not counseling his readers to seek some golden mean between two much righteousness and wisdom and too much wickedness and foolishness! Such an idea would fly in the face not only of the clear teachings of Scripture generally, but of Ecclesiastes in particular. Yet that has not prevented some, for obvious reasons, from leaping to such a conclusion.

It is the human way to want to be able to build with confidence a happy and prosperous future for ourselves in this life; in essence, to be in control of our destiny. Solomon has therefore introduced the verses now being looked at by an observation that our destiny in the world under the sun cannot be absolutely determined by whether we are righteous or wicked (7.15). And he has earlier noted that both the wise and the foolish are marked for death (2.15) and all are subject to life's often sudden deviations (3.1–11; 5.13–14; 6.1–2). So it is likely, as Iain Provan has suggested, that the Preacher is warning about some approaches to life's uncertainties that absolutely will not guarantee a good outcome (*The NIV Application Commentary, Ecclesiastes/Song of Solomon*, pp. 151–152).

"Do not be overly righteous, nor overly wise...." Solomon cannot be referring here to a sincere pursuit of righteousness as God in His mercy makes it possible. This is clearly an aberrant over the top idea that by a life of perfect purity one can guarantee a destiny of peace and prosperity in this present world. Even if such righteousness was a possibility, and it is not (Ecc 7.20; 1 Kgs 8.46; Prov 14.2–3; Psa 130.3), man is in no position to control his destiny here. And there is much pride and self-conceit in the effort. Man's wisdom, also, is inadequate for the task. We are not about to be as wise as God (Rom 11.33–34). As Paul observed many years later: "For since in the wisdom of God the world through wisdom did not know God, it pleased God through the foolishness of the message preached to save those who believe" (1 Cor. 1.21). God's wisdom is in the gospel of His grace, not in human righteousness and understanding.

"Do not be overly wicked, nor be foolish...." If our righteousness and wisdom are unable to guarantee a peaceful and prosperous course in this world, it is certain that wickedness and folly will not succeed. Solomon had already been down that road and found it "vanity and grasping for the wind" (Ecc 1.12–2.26). Paul warned about this course, too. "What shall we say then? Shall we continue in sin that grace may abound? Certainly not! How shall we who died to sin live any longer in it?" (Rom 6.1–2).

And what will be the consequence of these efforts to game divine providence? Self-destruction or an early death (7.16b, 17b). Though it is true that at times the righteous suffer grievous difficulties and the wicked walk pleasant paths, that is certainly not an absolute rule. So, both human self-righteousness and human wisdom, and the zealous pursuit of wickedness and folly, will end in disaster, likely here, and certainly in the hereafter.

How then are we to deal with the uncertainties with which life beneath the sun is fraught? Solomon had already answered that question in the Proverbs (9.10) and he repeats it here: "It is good that you grasp this, and also not remove your hand from the other; for he that fears God will escape them all" (7.18; note also 8.12–13). Reverencing and fearing God during all life's puzzling exigencies is the constant answer. It could not be better said than the Preacher had already written: "Trust in the Lord with all your heart, and lean not on your own understanding; in all your ways acknowledge Him, and He will direct [make smooth or straight] your paths" (Prov 3.5–6). There will be many circumstances in life here below that baffle us. But in all of them we need to turn our eyes heavenward and know with certainty that a gracious and benevolent God is at work in them all.

# The Fear of the Lord Is the Beginning of Wisdom

Solomon, having wrestled again unsuccessfully with the puzzling injustices which at times characterize life under the sun (7.15), has concluded anew that we must trust a righteous God to bring all things at last to equity (7.18; 3.14, 17).

Solomon's agonizing search for ultimate wisdom and knowledge, a dominant theme in Ecclesiastes, continues in these verses. His pursuit, though intense and determined, has brought him only frustration (1.18). His observation in Proverbs 10.27 was generally and proverbially correct ("The fear of the Lord prolongs days, but the days of the wicked will be shortened"), but the exceptions baffled him (Ecc 7.15; 8.14) as they did Asaph (Psa 73.1–14) and many others since.

In this section, the Preacher still finds value in practical wisdom and insight which he says provides greater strength than the raw power of ten rulers (v 19). But it is that wider and deeper wisdom that would explain the puzzling, paradoxical realities of life beneath the sun that eludes him (7.23–24). God spoke to this when He said by Isaiah: "'My thoughts are not your thoughts, nor are your ways My ways,' says the Lord. 'For as the heavens are higher than the earth, so are My ways higher than your ways and My thoughts than your thoughts'" (55.8–9). And Paul echoed

His words in Romans 11.33: "Oh, the depth of the wisdom and knowledge of God! How unsearchable are His judgments and His ways past tracing out!" So there is a sense in which Solomon was very wise and a more transcendent sense in which he was not, nor ever man shall be. The infinite wisdom of God is beyond him. Even wise men are imperfect. "For," as the Preacher has already said, "there is not a just man on earth who does good and does not sin" (7.20), a truth he had acknowledged long before (1 Kgs 8.46).

Sin stalks men like a wily seductress, a woman "whose heart is snares and nets, whose hands are like fetters" (7.26). In the Proverbs Solomon had sketched her out and warned young men of her treacherous way (7.1–23). Only the one whose aim is to please God will escape her. The mindless sinner will fall blindly into her trap.

These words and those that follow have caused Solomon to be charged by some with misogyny, a special prejudice against women. In his search for people of virtue, he says,

"One man among a thousand I have found, but a woman among all these I have not found" (7.27–28).

This may indeed be just a rhetorical device to stress the waywardness of the human race. In his defense, Solomon in the Proverbs portrayed wisdom as a woman and praises women as a blessing to their husbands (12.4; 18.22; 19.14) who are urged to find delight and joy in "the wife of [their] youth" (5.15–19; Ecc 9.9). There is also his Song of Songs in praise of married love. At the same time it must be said that his record with women was not a good one. He frequently speaks of the wretchedness of life with a contentious woman (19.13b; 21.9; 25.24). Indeed it was his deification of women that brought Solomon down (1 Kgs 11.1–9). No human being, not even a thousand, is capable of carrying the load that only God can bear.

In his book, *A Severe Mercy,* American author Sheldon Vanauken brings this lesson home. He and his wife, Davy, were married when both were agnostics and determined that they would mean everything to each other. Nothing and no one was to be allowed to breach that sacred covenant. Things changed, much to Vanauken's discomfort, when Davy began to be concerned about God. He reluctantly adjusted, joined Davy in a measure of faith, but still viewed life with Davy at the center, and on the side, God. Then tragedy struck when Davy was diagnosed with a fatal disease which in less than a year took her life. Herein lies the title of Vanauken's moving book. It was through the sickness and death of the wife to whom he was so devoted that God taught him a critical lesson in a "severe mercy": it can never be Davy, and God. It had to be God first, and then Davy.

And whose fault is it that there is not a single righteous man upon the earth who does good and does not sin? Solomon concludes: "Truly, this only I have found: that God made man upright, but they have sought out many schemes" (7.29). It is not then some inner corruption inherited from Adam that has brought us down, but our own willful ways. Fortunately for us, there is a man who did good and did not sin (Acts 10.38; 2 Cor 5.21), and it is in His innocent suffering that we can find our peace with God.

# Use Wisdom But Know Its Limitations

Ecclesiastes 8 seems to contain a clear unit of thought. Solomon begins by praising wisdom and ends by declaring its limitations in the face of life's baffling contradictions. His fruitless efforts to rationalize the inequities of life beneath the sun (8.10–14) continue. Such enigmas are only a challenge to those who believe that the world is ruled by a righteous God. Chaos and contradiction are not a bother to a non-believer. But this Preacher believes most fervently in a God of righteousness and justice (3.17; 11.9; 12.14) and for this reason the injustices of life are so troubling (3.16; 4.1). Solomon now expands more fully on the problem he raised in 7.15. Now he notes how the wicked who in their hypocrisy spent much time going to the "place of holiness" are buried with honor and praise (8.10). Unlike Shakespeare's observation in Julius Caesar that the good men do is often interred with their bones, it appears that the reverse is true and that a good funeral oration can expunge much iniquity. Additionally, the delay of any consequence for evil deeds further emboldens the wicked in their unrighteousness (v 11). Finally he mentions again the great inequity when it happens to just men "according to the work of the wicked" and to the wicked "according to the work of the righteous" (v 14).

The question being posed as the chapter begins is "how shall we respond to the unjust crookedness that surrounds us in this present world?" How are we to endure the constant oppression of the weak by the strong, the wickedness that inhabits high places where rulers seem to operate by the mere whim of power? Solomon recognizes that one may be tempted to rise up in rebellion against rulers that not only allow evil, but often instigate it. It is only human to desire some immediate and substantive correction to all this egregious unfairness. To such impulses he counsels prudence in the face of power beyond us but not beyond the power of God. We have neither the ability nor the prerogative to take care of such matters. Sheer Philistine power does not work divine purposes. As James wisely observed long afterward, "…the wrath of man does not produce the righteousness of God" (1.20).

Solomon offers several reasons for being submissive to rulers. The first is: "for the sake of your oath to God" (8.2, NKJV). There seemed to be an understanding in the wisdom literature that God expected His servants to be submissive to civil rulers. Solomon himself said as much in the Proverbs: "My son, fear the Lord and the king. Do not associate with those given to change ["rebellion"; NIV]; for their calamity will arise suddenly, and who knows the ruin those two can bring?" (24.21–22). Could this be an early statement of apostolic teaching: "Let every soul be subject to the governing authorities. For there is no authority except from God" (Rom. 13.1); "Therefore submit yourselves to every ordinance of man for the Lord's sake…" (1 Pet 2.13–14); "Fear God. Honor the king" (2.17)? The Preacher's additional reasons have to do with life-preserving prudence because of the king's absolute power and the danger of challenging him (Ecc 8.3–5a).

There is no question in the Preacher's mind that the grievous injustices under the sun have created great misery for its victims, but the wise will know that now is not the time for such matters to be adjudicated (8.5b–6). We know too little and have too little power to accomplish this. Our wisdom cannot penetrate the future and we have no power to control even the day of our death (8.7–8; 16–17).

So, what then is the answer? Foremost is to fear and trust the righteous God who knows all things and has the power to bring all things to a righteous end. Of this Solomon is certain, however things may now appear. "Though a sinner does evil a hundred times, and his days are prolonged, yet I surely know that it will be well with those who fear God, who fear before Him. But it will not be well with the wicked; nor will he prolong his days which are as a shadow, because he does not fear God" (8.12–13). Asaph would later come to the same conclusion (Psa 73).

And what should we do with the life and circumstance God has given us? Here, the Preacher repeats what he has said many times before (Ecc 2.24; 3.13, 22; 5.19; 7.14) and will say again in 9.7–9. "So I commended enjoyment, because a man has nothing better under the sun than to eat, drink, and be merry; for this will remain with him in his labor all the days of his life which God gives him under the sun" (8.15). Fear God, and receive the gifts he gives or withholds with gratitude and trust.

# Why Does God Delay So Long in Bringing Justice?

In Ecclesiastes 8, the Preacher concludes his wise counsels and observations with the frequently repeated warning that, however great may be the wisdom of men, it can never penetrate and explain God's work "under the sun" (8.16–17; cf. also 1.18; 3.11; 6.12; 7.23–24; Job 5.8–9; 26.14; Psa 145.3; 147.5; Rom 11.33–36). God's mind is infinite and His ways unsearchable. He is in heaven and we on the earth (Ecc 5.2) and "the secret things" still belong to Him alone (Deut 29.29). That is what we human beings need to know about the "unknowable." There are things which are not for us to know (Acts 1.6–7).

But I want to take a brief excursus to address a subject raised in 8.11: "Because sentence against an evil work is not executed speedily therefore the heart of the sons of men is fully set in them to do evil." Solomon is not naive about the grave injustices with which the world under the sun is beset. He raises the issue frequently. In this verse he ascribes much of human wickedness to the delay in punishment. It seems unlikely that Solomon is referring to the inaction of human rulers since they are seen as characteristically unconcerned about doing what is just (8.3–4). It seems far more probable that the reference is to God's delay in punishing the wicked and rewarding the righteous (7.15; 8.14). It is an age-old question (cf. Job 21.7–15; Psa 10.1–11; Psa 73; 2 Pet 3.3–10), and it has not gone away in the 21st century. Why does a righteous God allow such things? Why does He at times seem so far away and unconcerned about these grievous inequities? Why are we left to struggle in a world that sometimes makes no sense?

Of course, God could bring immediate justice to this world where Solomon himself observed that "there is not a just man on earth who does good and does not sin" (7.20). And how many of us would be left if such divine justice was meted out? But let us envision a world where sin and righteousness were immediately punished or rewarded. A world where the moment one contemplated an unholy thought or act a pain of such severity would strike the perpetrator that it would produce a scream of agony. And, also, every righteous act would bring exquisite pleasure, or result in immediate wealth and power. How many sinners would there be, and how many holy? We would all be like rats in a maze, seeking to avoid pain and diligently pursuing pleasure. And do you imagine that God would know what was truly in our hearts? The truth is that God is testing us in this broken world to see who we really are (3.18). In this way He tested Israel in the wilderness (Deut 8.2–3, 5). "Whom the Lord loves He chastens and scourges every son whom He receives" (Prov 3.11, as quoted in Heb 12.6).

C. S. Lewis gives some good insight on this subject in his *Screwtape Letters*, a fictional correspondence between Screwtape, a demon, and his nephew Wormwood. Screwtape says to Wormwood: "You must have wondered why the Enemy does not make more use of His power to be sensibly present to human souls in any degree He chooses and at any moment. But you now see that the Irresistible and the Indisputable are the two weapons which the very nature of His scheme forbids Him to use. Merely to override a human will (as His felt presence in any but the faintest and most mitigated degree would certainly do) would be for Him useless. He cannot ravish, He can only woo. ... He leaves the creature to stand up on its own legs—to carry out from the will alone duties which have lost all relish. ... He wants them to learn to walk and must therefore take away His hand; and if the will to walk is really there He is pleased even with their stumbles. Do not be deceived, Wormwood. Our cause is never more in danger than when a human, no longer desiring, but still intending, to do our Enemy's will, looks round upon a universe from which every trace of Him seems to have vanished, and asks why he has been forsaken, and still obeys" (*The Best of C.S. Lewis*, pp. 37–38). This is a frequent cry in the Psalms (Psa 42; 74; 88). Sufferings, like the puzzling mysteries of God's providence, can be an instrument of transformation and blessing in the Lord's hands. They drive us to trust in Him even when we do not understand. So the Psalmist said, "Before I was afflicted I went astray, but now I keep Your word. ... It is good for me that I have been afflicted, that I may learn Your statutes" (Psa 119.67, 71).

# Live Joyfully! *Ecclesiastes 9.1–12*

The Preacher concluded the eighth chapter with another of his oft-repeated observations that God's ways are inscrutable to men however wise (8.17). Job in his misery twice asks plaintively: "But where can wisdom be found? And where is the place of understanding?" (28.12, 20). And then answers his own question: "God understands its way, and He knows its place" (28.23). What then are we to do? He answers again: "Behold, the fear of the Lord, that is wisdom, and to depart from evil is understanding" (8.28). Only to the degree God has revealed His plan to us can we understand. The rest is shrouded and for that we must trust Him. This, too, is Solomon's unchanging answer to his repeated failures to fully grasp the nature of life under the sun.

One of the challenges in studying Ecclesiastes is the little emphasis put on God's benevolent providence for the righteous in all the pain and disappointments to which they are heir. There is a greater boldness in the New Testament on this subject (Rom 5.1–4; 8.28–39; Heb 12.5–11). In Ecclesiastes this truth is more implicit than stated, but in chapter nine it briefly surfaces. "For I considered all this [life's mysteries] in my heart," Solomon writes, "so that I could declare it all: that the righteous and the wise and all their works are *in the hand of God*" (9.1). Heretofore the Preacher has simply stressed that divine justice will at last be done (3.17;

8.12–13). Now he stresses that through all the storms and stresses that beset the righteous, they are being carried in the gracious arms of an almighty God. As Walter C. Kaiser, Jr. ably summed it up: "Our quest for identity, meaning, and an explanation of the presence of evil, injustice, and inequities in life must end where Solomon's did—-in the fact that God sits at the helm, ruling and overruling for good" (*Ecclesiastes: Total Life*, p. 94).

Nevertheless, no matter how true that is, the Preacher reemphasizes that such will not always be evident in what we experience here: "People know neither love nor hatred by anything they see that is before them" (9.1). He illustrates his point by proving that "all things come alike to all." The same thing happens to both the righteous and the wicked, the good and the sinner, the religious and the non-religious, the committed and uncommitted. They all go to the dead (9.2–3). As a result, some heedless men fill themselves up with evil until they are crazy with it (9.3; 1 Pet 4.3–5). And sin and madness surely do go together. We must be truly out of our minds if we think we can push the God who created us out of our lives and practice all the things that dishonor Him and injure others. So mindless people waste the one life they are given and plunge headlong into the death they know is coming and which will offer them no opportunity to change their destiny. Whatever they were, it is done (9.4–6). Solomon is not speaking here of annihilation (how could there be a judgment?), but of the fact that they will "nevermore have a share in anything done under the sun." The preciousness of life he has earlier stressed with a proverb: "But for him who is joined to the living there is hope, for a living dog is better than a dead lion" (9.4).

So, if the righteous are not to be distinguished from the wicked in their circumstances and their end, what should the righteous do? Should they allow their griefs and troubles to consume them, to brood and mope in pessimistic gloom? Solomon rejects this reaction as he has many times before (2.24; 3.12–13, 22; 5.18–19; 8.15), and here his exhortation to joy comes to a rather powerful conclusion (9.7–10). Don't just hope to live, he urges, live! Receive God's gifts gratefully and though you may not always have them, enjoy them when you do. Eat your food and savor it with gladness (Acts 2.46; the wine mentioned here is not a drug as in Proverbs 20.1; 23.29–35, but wholesome food as in Lamentations 2.11–12). Wear with gratitude the clothes you have been given and the soothing oil for your head, remembering that God has accepted your need of such things (9.7–8). And even more importantly, live joyfully with the mate God has blessed you with and give yourself heartily to your work (9.9–10).

And however can we do that? Because, though the race is not to the swift, nor the battle to the strong, nor bread to the wise, and death is certain (9.11–12), we are in the hands of a gracious and all-powerful God who loves us.

He leadeth me! O blessed tho't!
O words with heavenly comfort fraught!
Whate'er I do, where-e'er I be,
Still 'tis God's hand that leadeth me. (Joseph H. Gilmore, 1862)

# The Race Is Not to the Swift...

A more careful look at Ecclesiastes 9.11–12, one of the most noted passages in the book, would likely be helpful. "I returned and saw under the sun that—The race is not to the swift, nor the battle to the strong, nor bread to the wise, nor riches to men of understanding, nor favor to men of skill; but time and chance happen to them all." Solomon is not stating the rule here, but the exception, i.e., the race is not *always* to the swift, nor the battle *always* to the strong. One cannot count on the expected to always occur. Unexpected and unforeseeable events often take place, events beyond our control. So that, as Robert Burns observed, "The best laid plans of mice and men gang aft agley, and leave us naught but grief and pain for promised joy" (*Ode to a Field Mouse*). All people, the Preacher says, are subject to "time and chance." Today we might call this an "accident." Random and unexpected things happen in the world that God has cursed (Gen 3) and subjected to vanity (Rom 8.20). And, as the wise man further observes, all will die and none knows when (9.12). Indeed, it may seem that some die at an "evil" or unfortunate time. Some observers have thought this to be another explanation of why bad things happen to righteous people and good things to the wicked.

Yet Solomon has already made it clear that the times are in the hand of God (3.1–8). And in the beginning of this chapter he stressed that the righteous and the wise and their works are in God's hands (9.1). So, in spite of the uncertain picture that life beneath the sun paints for us, God in his providence will guide for good those who put their trust in Him (8.12). Illustrations that the race is not always to the swift, nor the battle to the strong are frequent in Scripture. In spite of all his efforts to disguise himself and frustrate divine prophecy, a random bowshot took Ahab down (1 Kgs 22.34). Goliath with his massive strength and armor should have easily overwhelmed David but a stone from a sling felled him (1 Sam 17.49). The Midianites should have easily defeated the army of Israel, but Gideon with only 300 men put them to flight (Jdg 7). God is the x-factor in all these events in which human strength and wisdom do not prevail. Jeremiah warns us pointedly about putting our trust in the wrong places: "Let not the wise man glory in his wisdom. Let not the mighty man glory in his might, nor let the rich man glory in his riches; but let him who glories glory in this, that he understands and knows Me, that I am the LORD, exercising loving-kindness, judgment, and righteousness in the earth" (9.23–24).

There is also a sense in which Solomon, in his own life, illustrated the principle that the wise and understanding do not always succeed. And perhaps, in a different way, the principle is seen in Jesus' prayer: "I thank you, Father, Lord of heaven and earth, that You have hidden these things from the wise and prudent and have revealed them to babes" (Matt 11.25). Paul also spoke to this when he wrote: "But God has chosen the foolish things of the world to put to shame the wise, and God has chosen the weak things of the world to put to shame the things which are mighty" (1 Cor 1.27).

So here, beneath the sun, things do not always happen as expected. Disappointments and inequities come often. But even in the Old Testament world, there was hope of a time beyond this

one when right would prevail. This theme is certainly not dominant in Ecclesiastes, but it is stated once explicitly (8.12) and often implied by references to ultimate divine judgment (3.17; 11.9;
12.14). This is clearly confirmed elsewhere: "But God will redeem
my soul from the power of the grave. For He will receive me" (Psa
49.15). "You will guide me with Your counsel and afterward receive me to glory" (Psa 73.24). "He will swallow up death forever,
and the Lord God will wipe away tears from all faces" (Isa 25.8).
"Your dead shall live; together with my dead body they shall
arise" (Isa 26.19). "And many of those who sleep in the dust of
the earth shall awake, some to everlasting life, some to everlasting
contempt" (Dan 12.2). "For I know that my Redeemer lives, and
He shall stand at last on the earth; and after my skin is destroyed,
this I know, that in my flesh I shall see God, whom I shall behold,
and not another" (Job 19.25–27).

Ecclesiastes may be candid about the present life's mysteries
and disappointments, but it is never cynical or hopeless.

# Wisdom Is Better than Strength: *Ecclesiastes 9.13–10.4*

In Ecclesiastes 9.13, the Preacher turns to a new section of thought: "This wisdom I have also seen under the sun...." Sidney Greidanus in his book *Preaching Christ from Ecclesiastes* sees these verses as among the most difficult to interpret and to preach. The difficulty arises because they seem to contain no overarching theme. They speak of wisdom and foolishness by the use of an illustrating story followed by a series of proverbs. The question immediately arises as to what kind of wisdom this is. Is it divine wisdom received by revelation or simply the practical prudence gathered from observing life's realities? Walter Kaiser, Jr. thinks it is divine wisdom (*Ecclesiastes: Total Life*, p. 105) while James E. Smith sees it as "worldly wisdom" (*Wisdom Literature & Psalms*, p. 792). There can be no doubt that in the wisdom literature true wisdom comes from "the fear of the Lord" (Job 28.28; Prov 1.7; 9.10; 15.33). And it may be accurately said that neither human counsel nor weapons of war are a match for the wise ways of God (Prov 21.30–31) because the battle always belongs to the Lord (1 Sam 17.47; 2 Chron 20.15). Yet in Ecclesiastes Solomon often sees wisdom as insight gathered from careful observation, and that seems to be the case here (9.13). Such wisdom is valuable in the practical affairs of daily life even though limited in its ability to answer transcendent questions (1.18; 7.11–12; 22–25; 8.16–17).

In the Preacher's story of the great king's assault on a little city, he demonstrates the superiority of wisdom over brute strength. The king with all the force on his side should have easily wiped out the tiny hamlet but the counsel of "a poor wise man" defeated him. Solomon's conclusion from his observations is that "wisdom is better than might" or "weapons of war" (9.16, 18). Armed with torches and trumpets, Gideon with his 300 overwhelmed a huge Midianite army (Jdg 7.19–22). But the story provides another side to the life of wisdom. Though the poor wise man delivered his city, he went unremembered (v 15). Indeed it is usual for a poor man's wisdom to be despised and his words unheeded (v 16) because he is bereft of the pomp and circumstance of power. Nevertheless, Solomon concludes that "the words of the wise heard in quiet are better than the shouting of a ruler among fools" (9.17). But again the Preacher states a countervailing truth that the good of great wisdom can be undone by a single sinner (v 18b).

There is no greater illustration of these observations of Solomon's than the Son of God Himself? He came in such a meek and quiet way. Of Him Isaiah wrote, "He will not cry out, nor raise His voice in the street. A bruised reed He will not break, and smoking flax He will not quench" (42.2–3; Matt 12.19–20). Jesus certainly was poor and without carnal credentials (Luke 9.58; Mark 6.2–3). And yet He was wisdom and truth incarnate (John 1.14; 14.6). He saved not just a city, but the whole world (John 3.16; Heb 2.9), yet still remains unremembered and unheard by most. His death was the means and His gospel the power to save all men (Rom 1.16). The power of this world is nothing compared to His (Eph 1.20–22). And it is, at last, His wisdom that will prevail.

In chapter 10, the Preacher extends his comments in 9.18 and applies them to an individual life with his "fly in the ointment" proverb. Just as the perfumer's carefully prepared ointment with all its potential for a wonderful aroma is completely canceled by a few dead flies, so the influence of a life of great wisdom is destroyed by one act of folly. This bears some similarity to our "there is no fool like an old fool." Examples of this are replete. Asa, the king of Judah, walked humbly with God for most of his reign, but his angry response to a rebuke from God's prophet overshadowed his earlier wisdom and courage (2 Chron 16). Jehoshaphat, who succeeded Asa, fell into the same blunder. After a life of trust in God, a very unwise alliance with Ahaziah, the king of Israel, brought rebuke from God and the destruction of all his works (2 Chron 20.35–37). Uzziah, a later king of Judah, also began in a wonderful way and ended his long reign in disease and disgrace (2 Chron 26.16–21).

So it is that a wise man's heart is always pointed in the right direction while a fool's heart is perverse and rebellious (10.2). Consequently, what is in the heart of a fool is always revealed by the choices he makes and the roads he takes (10.3). Point made. It is in our hearts that the direction of our lives is decided, whether to wisdom and righteousness or to folly and disaster.

# Wise Counsel in a Dangerous World

In Ecclesiastes 10.4, Solomon returns to counsel already given. He has earlier urged respect for rulers and submission to their commands not only out of compliance with the will of God but out of good sense. Power lies with the king (8.2–4). He returns now to counsel wise behavior in the face of folly in high places (10.4–7, 16–20). He still says that it is ill advised to challenge an angry ruler since it will only exacerbate a dangerous situation (10.4; 8.3). This was the counsel of the Proverbs: "A soft answer turns away wrath but a harsh word stirs up anger" (15.1) and "By long forbearance a ruler is persuaded, and a gentle tongue breaks a bone" (25.15).

This counsel is especially appropriate in view of the political craziness and corruption which the Preacher sees as a widespread evil. Fools like Haman in Esther's day are set in high places to rule not out of justice, but out of their own arrogant self-interest. Rehoboam sought the counsel not of the aged wise but of some heady young fools (1 Kgs 12). The affairs of state are turned upside down. Servants ride on horses while princes walk. Those ill-equipped to rule are elevated while those most likely to govern well are kept out of office (Ecc 10.6–7). In spite of all the progress often ascribed to modern days, it appears at times that nothing has changed.

In the latter part of chapter 10, Solomon returns to his theme with a contrasting woe and blessing. "Woe to you, O land, when your king is a child, and your princes feast in the morning!" (10.16). His point is not that the king is a literal child but one who is childish and indifferent to anyone's interest but his own. And it is not the eating habits of the princes he decries so much as that they are in office to feed themselves not their subjects. And in contrast: "Blessed are you, O land, when your king is the son of nobles, and your princes feast at the proper time—for strength and not for drunkenness!" (10.17). Here too, the point is not so much noble birth as the nobility of a wise and selfless disposition, and not so much the eating habits of the princes as their inclination to seek strength in their work and not dissipation. But because of the previously stated indulgence and lazy indifference at the top, the state of the people falls into ruin like a decaying house with a leaky roof (10.18). All this while those in power revel and cynically declare, "A feast is made for laughter, and wine makes merry; but money answers everything" (10.19). And as Walter C. Kaiser, Jr. surmises, that spirit may come to infect the populace at large (*Ecclesiastes: Total Life*, p. 112).

Still, a bit surprisingly, Solomon warns that in the face of such corruption in high places, it is unwise to speak against the king or his rich associates even in a corner because the word will inevitably get out, much to your disadvantage (10.20).

That God has allowed the rule of such corrupt individuals has been a challenge to His worshippers, especially in view of Daniel's declaration that "the Most High rules in the kingdoms of men, and gives it to whomever He chooses" (4.25). Certainly this is true, but it must be remembered that God's providence in the matter of rulers is governed by His even higher purpose to have a people for His own possession. It is clearly not God's eternal purpose to transform the political, economic and social institutions of the world, but the hearts of the people. Jesus is a perfect demonstration of this truth. He came to seek and to save those who are lost (Luke 19.10). And it was never envisioned that such should be universal for "narrow is the gate and difficult the way which leads to life, and there are few that find it" (Matt 7.14).

In the midst of his discourse on the dangers associated with matters of state, Solomon introduces some proverbs that speak to the more ordinary dangers which must be met with wisdom (10.8–15). The proverbs are not absolute, but provisional. If one is not careful, he will fall into the pit he has dug or in breaking through a wall be bitten by a serpent or when working with great stones be severely injured (10.8–9; Prov 26.27). When splitting wood, one must be especially careful and not waste valuable energy because the axe has not been properly sharpened. All these precautions speak to simple common sense that will bring success rather than tragedy in any endeavor.

Verses 11–15 are another intervening series of proverbs contrasting the wise man and the fool. The foolish babbler whose tongue wags heedlessly is said to be as dangerous as an uncharmed serpent (10.11). The words of the wise are a blessing, while the fool's mouth intoxicates him into a wild explosion of utter madness (10.12–13). A fool talks endlessly about things of which he knows nothing and is even ignorant of obvious simplicities—the way to town (10.14–15). For the fool, the world surely is a very dangerous place.

# The Folly of Playing It Safe

In Ecclesiastes 11, Solomon continues his admonitions to wise living, now in the face of life's uncertainties. As he has frequently reminded us, we cannot know what will come after us (3.22; 6.12; 8.7; 10.14). God's providence is shrouded and beyond human wisdom to fathom or predict. The race is not always to the swift or the battle to the strong (9.11). In the previous chapter he spoke of the risks that life's ordinary activities hold (10.8–9). The uncertainty as to the outcome of one's labors has caused some to avoid all risk by doing nothing. Life at its best is not risk free. All worthy efforts and investments do not always yield their intended results. But doing nothing is a guarantee of failure by default. To drive home the foolishness of such mindless caution, the Preacher gives an imperative call to bold action in spite of so many things being outside our control.

*"Cast [send out] your bread upon the waters, for you will find it after many days. Give a portion to seven, and also to eight, for you do not know what evil will be upon the earth"* (11.1–2). These verses have been traditionally understood to refer to the ultimate reward one will receive for being generous to the unfortunate. This may indeed be true, but this exhortation is far more likely to be urging commercial ventures spread widely in several directions with a long-term view of success. The evil mentioned does not speak of immorality but of unforeseen misfortunes, which cannot be

anticipated or controlled. *"If the clouds are full of rain, they empty themselves upon the earth; and if a tree falls to the south or the north, in the place where the tree falls, there it shall lie"* (11.3). The English proverb that speaks to the same issue says that one should not put all his eggs in one basket.

In verse 4, Solomon makes the same point, illustrating it with farming rather than commerce. *"He who observes the wind will not sow, and he who regards the clouds will not reap."* Farming is often viewed by the uninitiated as a work of stress-less peace. But a farmer deals with so many variables—the weather, violent storms, drought and flood, insects and disease, and then there are the vagaries of the market. It is a wonder he has the courage to invest so much money and labor into his crops. So the Preacher warns that *"He who observes the wind will not sow, and he who observes the clouds will not reap"* (11.4). There are so many things the farmer does not know. He does not *"know the way of the wind, or how the bones grow in the womb of her who is with child."* Like all of us, he does *"not know the works of God who makes everything"* (11.5). But one thing he knows for sure is that if he does not sow, he certainly will not reap. Therefore Solomon urges: *"In the morning sow your seed, and in the evening do not withhold your hand; for you do not know which will prosper, either this or that, or whether both alike will be good"* (11.6).

Is this all there is to these sayings, just prudent counsel for business and farming? It is true that the Preacher has earlier urged that *"Whatever your hand finds to, do it with your might…"* (9.10), but surely there is a greater application to be made here. In Jesus' parable of the talents, He warns against doing nothing, in fear of risk. The man who was given one talent to invest for his master hid it in the ground for fear of losing it. His lord called him "a wicked and lazy servant" (Matt 25.24–26). As followers of Jesus, we are called upon to speak the gospel message to all, knowing from the start that not all will receive it and that some who do will not continue (Matt 13.18–23). And we are not the first to have such a commission (Isa 6.8–13; Ezek 33.30–33). Should we therefore do nothing because many will not listen?!

There are risks in serving Christ and we need to be willing to take them. Some risks are obviously foolish, but those we take for the Lord's sake are not (1 Cor 15.58). The apostle Paul was in constant risk during his life of preaching. The roads were not safe; the rivers were not safe; his own people were not safe; the Gentiles were not safe; the cities were not safe; the sea was not safe; his own brethren were not safe. He did not always have enough sleep, enough to eat or enough clothing to keep himself warm (2 Cor 11.23–27). But none of these things ever deterred him (Acts 20.22–24). They must not deter us. As the Lord Himself has said, we must risk the loss of everything in order to be His disciple (Luke 14.33).

# Finding a Place to Stand

As we come to the final chapter of Ecclesiastes, we hope our readers will allow a brief excursus. Archimedes, the great Greek mathematician and scientist who discovered the principal of the lever, once said, "Give me a place to stand and I will move the earth." Solomon in this great book was searching for a spiritual place to stand. In all his examination of life under the sun, he found no solid immovable thing on which to plant his feet. Everything here is brittle with uncertainty and bounded by brevity. Life on earth is a fragile thing and our stay on it is destined to be terribly short. And Solomon is not the first or only one to point this out. Job saw this early when he wrote, "Man who is born of woman is of few days and full of trouble. He comes forth like a flower and fades away; He flees like a shadow and does not continue" (14.1–2). Moses observed the same in his memorable psalm: "The days of our lives are seventy years; and if by reason of strength they are eighty years, yet their boast is only labor and sorrow; for it is soon cut off, and we fly away" (Psa 90.10).

Solomon's father, David, who lived just seventy years, echoed this truth: "Lord, make me to know my end, and what is the measure of my days, that I may know how frail I am. Indeed, you have made my days as handbreadths, and my age as nothing before You; Certainly every man at his best state is but vapor. Surely every man walks about like a shadow; Surely they busy themselves in vain;

He heaps up riches, and does not know who will gather them" (Psa 39.4–6). Even James, in the New Testament, adds his voice to this truth: "For what is your life? It is even a vapor that appears for a little time and then vanishes away" (Jas 4.14b). As David says and the New Testament attests, we are just passing through this world as strangers and pilgrims (Psa 39.12; 1 Pet 2.11). We cannot stay here and we cannot keep anything we find here.

C. S. Lewis, in the second book of his mythical space trilogy Perelandra, imagines his character Doctor Ransom transported to Venus. There he finds himself on vegetative islands which undulate with the sea beneath them and mountains are regularly transformed into valleys and valleys into mountains. Lewis intended his imagery to suggest a happy prospect, but it seems to be a perfect illustration of life in our world. Things are always moving and changing, in a constant state of flux. There is no fixed ground here. There is no immutable thing upon which to rest one's life and hope. Our own lives may indeed be brief, but even the universe itself has no permanence. "You, Lord, in the beginning laid the foundation of the earth, and the heavens are the work of your hands. They will perish but You remain; and they will all grow old like a garment; like a cloak You will fold them up and they will be changed. But You are the same, and Your years will not fail" (Psa 102.25–27; as quoted in Heb 1.10–12). And in these same verses, the answer to Solomon's quest is found. The fixed and unchanging foundation upon which we may stand with confidence is beyond this world. It is the eternal and unchanging God who will always be the same. This is the answer that Moses gives in the 90th Psalm: "Lord, You have been our dwelling place in all generations" (90.1). It is the answer that David gives in Psalm 39: "And now, Lord, what do I wait for? My hope is in You" (v 7).

As might be expected, the same is said of God's word. "Heaven and earth will pass away, but My words will by no means pass away" (Matt 24.35). Peter, quoting Isaiah 40.6–8, writes of "... the word of God which lives and abides forever, because all flesh is as grass, and all the glory of man as the flower of the grass. The grass withers, and the flower falls away, but the word of the Lord endures forever. Now this is the word which by the gospel was preached to you" (1 Pet 1.23–25). The words of God, like Himself, are eternal and will transcend this world of time and space. Upon that word we can rest secure, for "He who promised is faithful" (Heb 11.23).

God's kingdom also is transcendent. He will indeed yet shake heaven and earth into nothing, but we have received a kingdom which cannot be shaken (Heb 12.26–28). We have found our place to stand. It is on the Christ who "is the same, yesterday, today and forever" (Heb 13.8). Solomon is certainly vindicated in both the New Testament and human experience. The world, as it is, is always moving and changing under our feet. We need to be prepared for the one that will come afterward.

# Rejoice ... and Remember: *Ecclesiastes 11.7–10*

In this significant book, Solomon is in search of the ultimate meaning and purpose of life. He has not found it anywhere in the material world, the world "under the sun." All there is vanity and emptiness—they neither last nor satisfy the human spirit (Ecc 2.21–23; 5.10–11; 6.7–9). Yet, in spite of the fact that the physical world and all of human prudence will not yield the answer to his quest, he commends the value of both for their present usefulness (2.24; 3.12–13; 5.18–19; 7.14; 8.15; 9.7–9). They are to be enjoyed and rejoiced in as gifts from God (2.24; 3.13, 22; 5.19). This latter theme has followed along with the first throughout the book. And now for the seventh and final time, he calls upon his readers to "rejoice" (life and its attendant blessings, however fleeting and uncertain, are to be received gratefully). When esteemed as what life is all about, they become poisonous, but when held loosely, they are wholesome. In these now concluding verses of the wise man's book, these two themes of joy and wisdom are intertwined.

There are those who see the godly life as one in which the joy has been sucked out in order to find it in the afterlife. Solomon says otherwise: *"Truly the light is sweet, and it is pleasant for the eyes to behold the sun. But if a man lives many years* [let him rejoice—

ASV, NIV, ESV] *in all of them*" (11.7–8a). And the New Testament makes it eminently clear that such a view is mistaken: "For the kingdom of God is not eating and drinking but righteousness, peace and joy in the Holy Spirit" (Rom 14.17); "But the fruit of the Spirit is love, joy, peace, longsuffering, kindness..." (Gal 5.22); and "Now the God of hope fill you with all joy and peace in believing..." (Rom 15.13).

Life, when it is sweet and the sun is shining, should be enjoyed, but such good days must be received with the realization that they do not last forever and difficult days, "days of darkness" are ahead (11.7–8). These dark days seem to speak of the debilities of old age and the death to which they lead. Such forces are no friend to life and joy and are seen in the New Testament as a curse and an enemy (Rom 8.20; 1 Cor 15.25–26), something which sin has caused God to unleash in the world (Gen 3.17–19). They are not in the purest sense "natural" to the ultimate divine purpose but are, in and of themselves, vanity and emptiness (11.8b). They will at last be conquered in Christ who can make even the dark days meaningful (2 Cor 4.16–17; Phil 1.20–21).

As his exhortations are concluding, the wise man addresses himself to the young. *"Rejoice, O young man in your youth, and let your heart cheer you in the days of your youth; walk in the ways of your heart, and in the sight of your eyes..."* (11.9a). There is no reason to conclude that this appeal to joy for the young is any less genuine than all those that have preceded. It certainly is not cynical. Young people should enjoy their youthful days when they are at their physical and intellectual peak. They should not behave as if decrepit. Youth is valued in the Scripture for its special qualities (Prov 20.20; 1 John 2.13–14). It only becomes toxic when it is made the end all and be all of life (11.10b). This is seen in those who try to "cosmetize" themselves into eternal youth.

As someone has observed about age, "Never have so many lied so much about so little."

Solomon's concern for the young is not new. It is evident in the Proverbs. He is an old man who blundered into many a dead end and longs to help the young avoid the same pitfalls. No one needs Solomon's long view of life under the sun nor will be more benefited by it than the young. They stand poised with most of their life yet before them. Youth can be so intoxicating, so filled with self-confidence and naive optimism. Their joy in life must be tempered by the realization that their present choices have transcendent consequences. They cannot live life with wild abandon, sow wild oats and then pray for a crop failure (Gal 6.8). They like all others will be held to account in the highest court of all. But consequences of our choices do not all come due then. They can bear some bitter fruit while we live. So Solomon urges the young to conduct themselves in wisdom so as to remove sorrow from their heart and evil from their flesh (11.10). He refers here to the mental and emotional anguish and the physical tragedy which sin by its very nature brings. Because we were created by God for a very high destiny (Gen 1.27), we will never function well on pride and self-will. We will only find joy when we are guided by divine wisdom.

# Remember God When You Are Young

Solomon's advice to the young has been clear: Rejoice in your youthful days, the days of strength and vitality. They are God-given. The way of God is not to dismiss the inherent joys of youth—the physical energy, the mental keenness, the anticipation, the delight in life's newness and promise. Nothing that is pure is withheld. So treasure them and thank God for them, but reflect soberly on two things. First, they pass swiftly and are not therefore the essence of life. Second, though not what life is all about, they must not be lived heedlessly, for we will be called to give account to God for every moment of them. Live joyfully, but soberly, he urges, because there are transcendent consequences for the choices made in youth. The inexorable law that you will reap what you sow is still operative and those who sow to the flesh will of the flesh reap corruption (Gal 6.8). So the joy of youth must be sobered by two coming realities: the dark days of old age and death, and the judgment which will follow (11.7–10). It is with these two things in mind that Solomon presses upon the young what must be their overriding present, not just future, concern. And it is upon these two things, death and judgment, that the rest of the book will be focused.

*"Remember now your Creator in the days of your youth"* (12.1). That is imperative first of all because it is God, not ourselves, who created us (Psa 100.4) and He must therefore be looked on with

reverential awe (5.1–7). His purposes for us must therefore override our own whims. To do otherwise is to war against our own intrinsic divinely ordered nature. The heady days of youth can make one forget this very significant truth. We can forget that we are not self-designed, but created by God for His purpose and not our own. We can also forget that we are not self-sufficient, but creatures entirely dependent on the One who created us. We have nothing that God has not given to us (1 Cor 4.7). And that is true because in Him "we live and move and have our being" (Acts 17.28). Our very breath comes from Him (Job 12.10). For this reason we need to receive His gifts with grateful thanks and due reverence. To fail to do so is the ultimate stupidity whether in youth or old age (Rom 1.21).

There is a second reason why we should remember God in our youth. It is because it is in those days that our eventual character is being formed. As poet William Wordsworth once accurately observed, "The child is father to the man." Yesterday influences today and today will influence tomorrow. It is in those days that critical decisions are made which will influence for good or for ill the rest of our lives. Habits can be formed that will carve deep ruts in our temperament that may be very difficult to root out in later life, but could have been easily checked in youth.

But to truly remember our Creator involves far more than an occasional glance in His direction. is HisIt means to take Him most seriously until who He is and what He wills becomes the central focus of our lives.

Those of us who are older have frequently made a serious mistake in our attitude toward young people. We have treated youth as a parenthesis in life that must be gotten over before a serious spiritual challenge will be accepted. That is not true and it is certainly not the biblical view. It is not Solomon's. We celebrate the faith and moral courage of a very young Daniel who was snatched up in a military raid and carried far away from his family to Babylon. We laud the spiritual fortitude of a teenaged Joseph who survived slavery and seduction to trust the faithfulness of God. Yet we do not place before today's young people the opportunity to live heroically for Christ.

Yet the Preacher's view is that the most serious attention must be paid to God when young, *"before the difficult days come."* These are the years concerning which you will say, *"I have no pleasure in them."* His reference is to the days of advanced years when the body is falling into disrepair, the mind is no longer keen and death is in full view (2 Sam 19.35). This is a bad time to reserve for thinking about God when your faculties are in serious decline and you are hamstrung with many a long established adverse habit. It's not that God will not forgive, but the chances that your heart has grown too hard to respond are far greater. And there are the consequences of delay. God was merciful to Manasseh who repented of all his wickedness in later life, but the fallout for his sons and the nation was awful (2 Kgs 21.11–16; 2 Chron 33.1–13). It does not always happen that people are exposed to and take God seriously in their young years, but it is obviously the course of great wisdom.

# Before the Dark and Difficult Days Come: *Ecclesiastes 12.1–7*

Solomon's concern for youth to remember their Creator was because of the coming ravages of old age (11.8; 12.1). Advancing years would make it even more difficult to overcome the intervening heart-hardening habit of ignoring God. Neither would the mind-dulling consequences of advancing years facilitate serious thoughts about the Almighty. Death is coming with its preface of growing mental and physical decay. Implicit in the Preacher's counsel is the wisdom and the need for us to give God the best years of our lives and not waste our choice days in vanity while offering Him the dying end. We have watched enough people who burn the candle at both ends and offer God the smoke. One thing is certain. If we give our best years to the Lord, they will serve to cheer us in the dark years of our dotage.

The difficult days, the Preacher says, will be devoid of pleasure (12.1b). Does this suggest the case of those who spent their strong and vital days in physical indulgence and now their bodily incapacity has ended all that and left them burnt out hulks? Of this Solomon has been warning all along—the foolishness of investing one's life in the temporary and unsatisfying vanities beneath the sun. Such days will indeed be dark, with nothing to remember with joy and nothing to look forward to with hope. This surely must be some of the author's perspective, for it certainly is not the dominant view of old age in the New Testament. Witness Paul's words in 2 Corinthians 4.16–18: "Therefore we do not lose heart. Even though our outward man is perishing, yet our inward man is being renewed day by day. For our light affliction, which is for a moment, is working a far more exceeding and eternal weight of glory." Even Solomon in the Proverbs seems to exalt advanced years: "The silver-haired head is a crown of glory, if it is found in the way of righteousness" (16.31) and "the splendor of old men is their gray head" (20.29). Job agrees: "Wisdom is with aged men and with length of days, understanding" (12.12).

Yet there is no question that old age, moving from strength and independence to dependent frailty, has its challenges for everyone. The strongly figurative words of Ecclesiastes 12.2–7 have been a challenge to interpreters and variously understood, but one thing is certain—they speak of the disabilities of advanced years and ensuing death.

Old age is first compared to the darkness and storm of wintry days. In youth the sunshine returns after the rain. Sorrows are infrequent and soon forgotten, but in the winter of life the burdens seem to come one after another (12.2). In the verses following (12.3–5), the figure of a decaying house is used to describe the decay of the human body.

The "keepers of the house" (the arms and hands) grow weak and trembly. The "strong men" (the legs) become feeble and bent. The "grinders" (teeth) make eating difficult because "they are few." "Those that look through the windows (the eyes) grow dim." Vision is diminished and impaired. "The doors are shut in the street"—possibly the mouth (Mic 7.5) which, lacking teeth, falls in upon itself. "One rises at the sound of a bird"—sleep is light and easily interrupted. One rises early though there are no duties to fulfill. "All the daughters of music are brought low"—the voice is weakened and hearing greatly diminished. "Also they are afraid of heights and terrors in the way"—greatly reduced strength makes heights once easily navigated to be dangerous and familiar paths once walked with ease an occasion of stumbling. "When the almond tree blossoms"—the fading of the hair's color to white (the almond tree blossoms white before it puts on leaves). "The grasshopper is a burden" ("drags himself along" NASB)—difficult but may refer to the bent and awkward gait with which the elderly move. "And desire fails"—the enjoyment of youthful pleasures is gone. God's gifts to the young and strong—work, food and sexual love have faded (2 Sam 19.35; 1 Kgs 1.2–4). This is our destiny if we live a normal life, and therefore our vital responsibilities to our Creator must ideally be met long before these days come.

Now Solomon is explicit. "For man goes to his eternal home and the mourners go about the street." We are on a journey to death when life here and the opportunity to remember our Creator and acknowledge and submit to His will and purpose for us is over. And so again the Preacher urges the young to act swiftly before death cuts off all opportunity. In 12.6, Solomon may be describing death as the loss of all light and water: light because the silver cord which holds the lamp is severed and the bowl which holds the oil is broken, and water because the pitcher to receive the water at the fountain is shattered and the wheel that draws water at the well is stilled.

So man goes to his eternal home (12.5b). The body returns to the dust from whence it came and the spirit to God who gave it (12.7). And so much to do before then.

# Solomon's Search Ended: *Ecclesiastes 12.8*

The Preacher ends his study of life under the sun just as it began (1.2). Solomon's book about his search for ultimate meaning is not a journal record of his mistaken conclusions on the road to the real answer. He knew that answer and stated it in the beginning. The physical universe has its usefulness as the arena where we learn that it contains within itself nothing upon which to build our lives or find a sense of ultimate meaning or purpose. There are good and joyful things in this world that are to be credited to a good and merciful Creator (2.24; 3.13; 5.19; 9.7–9), but they are uncertain and may, like our lives, be suddenly snatched away. Youth does not last forever (11.10b). In the end, in spite of all our wisdom and carefulness, death inevitably stalks and finds us (9.11–12; 12.6–7). It reminds us again that the world of which the Preacher speaks is the cursed world of Genesis 3 and not the perfect one of Genesis 2. As the apostle Paul observed, God has subjected the creation to vanity, but He has done so "in hope," hope that all the emptiness of this present world would cause us to lift our eyes heavenward (Rom 8.20).

Many students of this great book have concluded that the seemingly dark sayings of the Preacher were due to the fact that he had no concept of the hereafter. That appears to be the general consensus even among some conservative scholars. "The Old Testament thought that death was the end" (Sidney Greidanus, *Preaching Christ from Ecclesiastes*, p. 293); "From the New Testament perspective there are eternal implications bound up with our present decisions. Qohelet does not know of these..." (Iain Provain, *The NIV Application Commentary—Ecclesiastes/Song of Solomon*, p. 321); "Koheleth has no thought of afterlife in his picture of death in 12.1–7" (David Hubbard, *Ecclesiastes, Song of Solomon*, p. 243). But not all conservative students of the book are of that persuasion. "Death is the returning of the body to the *dust*. The *spirit* (the principle of responsible, intelligent life) has a distinct destiny. The teacher is pointing to life after death" (Michael Eaton, *New Bible Commentary*, p. 618). Walter C. Kaiser, Jr. is of a similar persuasion (*Ecclesiastes: Total Life*, p. 122). We believe that the evidence found in the book reflects this latter view.

First, it is evident that it is Solomon's belief that justice is not brought to completion under the sun: "Moreover I saw under the sun: in the place of judgment wickedness was there and in the place of righteousness, iniquity was there" (3.16). Indeed, here on earth, proper rewards are reversed: "There is a just man who perishes in his righteousness, and there is a wicked man who prolongs his life in wickedness" (7.15); "There is a vanity which occurs on earth, that there are just men to whom it happens according to the work of the wicked; again, there are wicked men to whom it happens according the work of the righteous, I said this also is vanity" (8.14). And yet it is clear that the Preacher believes that God will at last, beyond this world of time and space, bring all things to equity. "I said in my heart, God shall judge the righteous and the wicked, for there is a time there for every purpose and for every work" (3.17); "Though a sinner does evil and hundred times, and his days are prolonged, yet I surely know that it will be well with those that fear God, who fear before Him. But it will not be well with the wicked; nor will he prolong his days because he does not fear before God" (8.12–13). And all this without adding the words of the book's closing verse (12.14). The context of these passages gives additional support to the idea of afterlife in the language of 12.5b: "For man goes to his eternal home" and that of 12.7: "Then the dust will return to the earth as it was and the spirit will return to God who gave it."

Other Old Testament passages support this view: Genesis 5.26; Job 14.13–17; 19.25–27; Psalms 16.9–11; 17.15; Hosea 6.2; 13.14; Isaiah 26.19; Daniel 12.1–2; et. al.

What might be said with certainty is that the Old Testament writers did not have the clear view of the life to come seen in New Testament writers who were, after all, the recipients of the fullness of truth that came through the Son of God Himself.

So, in short, Solomon is telling us: Everyone take careful note. Wealth or health or great wisdom or celebrity or long life or many children or all combined, however pleasant for the moment, cannot bring ultimate peace and joy. It is not here in things resident in this material planet that true fulfillment can be found. That treasure can only be found by looking above and beyond the sun. It is our tragedy that it takes us so long to figure that out. Solomon is trying so earnestly to help us.

# The Answer To What Life Is All About: *Ecclesiastes 12.9–14*

Solomon's record of his search for life's ultimate purpose has run like a turbulent river, full of cataracts, whirlpools and rushing currents. His epilogue in contrast is like a quiet stream, calm with certitude and finality. Many have questioned that it is by the same author and speculate that it is the work of some unknown editor because it is written in the third person and the past tense. This view is not definitive because some Old Testament prophets wrote of themselves in the third person (Isa 20.2; 37.21; Dan 2.14; 10.1) and yet their authorship is unquestioned. So the last words of the book seem to be a natural summation of what the Preacher has been saying all along and are clearly harmonious with the rest of Ecclesiastes.

*"And moreover, because the Preacher was wise, he still taught the people knowledge...."* Solomon begins his conclusion with an explanation of the purpose and nature of his words and the reason they were upright and true. The Preacher's research behind his conclusions had been wide and deep. From that experience he taught the people, to give them knowledge to guide their lives to a happy rather than a disastrous end. His words were not only acceptable (delightful) but also true because they originated from "one Shepherd," that is, they were inspired by God (Psa 23; 80.1).

*"...yes, he pondered and sought out and set in order many prov-erbs."* The proverbial wisdom of Solomon is well known (1 Kgs 4.32). He has been diligent in Ecclesiastes to give wise counsel about how to live in a world full of uncertainty and injustice. But to get an answer to the meaning of life, he has had to reach above the sun.

*"The Preacher sought to find acceptable words; and what was written was upright—words of truth."* It is evident that Solomon not only determined to speak words that were true but words that were "acceptable" (pleasing). The truth of God must be taught but it can be taught in such a harsh and unappealing way as to make it harder to accept. Even Paul, who could speak plainly when necessary, addresses this matter in several places: "gentle to all, able to teach, patient" (2 Tim 2.24); "in humility" (2.25); "with all longsuffering and teaching" (2 Tim 4.2). Our words should be "with grace, seasoned with salt" (Col 4.6). Many are not going to accept the truth of God, however taught, but we should not make it unnecessarily unappealing by the words we choose and the attitude we manifest. "Let all that you do be done with love" (1 Cor 16.14).

*"The words of the wise are like goads, and the words of scholars [masters of assemblies] are like well-driven nails...."* The words of the wise, because they are true, are like goads to those who receive them. A goad was a sharp-pointed prod with which to move animals to their intended work or keep them going in the right direction. Wise words are often painful but it is a good pain that urges us to needed action or corrects an untoward course. We should not "kick against the pricks" (Acts 26.14). Words of wisdom are also like well-driven nails, words that give us certitude and a solid foundation on which to live and build. It was just that which was the object of Solomon's search in Ecclesiastes.

*"And further, my son, be admonished by these. Of making many books there is no end, and much study is a weariness of the flesh."* The library of human wisdom is ever expanding and always without answers to life's most critical questions. They lead only to weariness and emptiness. The answer to the meaning of life cannot be found "beneath the sun" nor can men discover it by searching. It must be given to them by God.

*"Let us hear the conclusion of the matter: Fear God and keep His commandments. For this is man's all. For God will bring every work into judgment, including every secret thing, whether good or evil."* We may not be able to understand and explain all the mysteries of God's providential working here below, but we must not let that steal from us our reverence for and trust in Him as our Creator (Psa 100.3). We are creatures designed by Him and He alone knows the purpose of our lives and what will give us ultimate fulfillment. Solomon states the whole intent of our being in these simple words: "Fear God and keep His commandments."

And it is imperative that we fulfill it because the God who knows all things is going to bring each of us into judgment, and the justice which has eluded us or we have escaped here will be achieved in a world beyond the sun (3.17; 8.12–13; 11.9). And even Solomon knew that none of us would keep God's commandments perfectly (9.20). So there is an implication of grace even in this sober charge. There is hope truly for sinners who set their heart to worship Him and do His will. But the future is bleak indeed for those who do not.

What a great book is Ecclesiastes! It warns us about all the things life is not about. And while speaking candidly about this broken world, the Preacher guides us surely to our God-given purpose.

# *Also by Paul Earnhart*

## Invitation to a Spiritual Revolution
*Studies in the Sermon on the Mount*

Few preachers have studied the Sermon on the Mount as intensively or spoken on its contents so frequently and effectively as the author of this work. His excellent and very readable written analysis appeared first as a series of articles in *Christianity Magazine.* By popular demand it is here offered in one volume so that it can be more easily preserved, circulated, read, reread and made available to those who would not otherwise have access to it. Foreword by Sewell Hall. 173 pages, $9.99 (PB).

## Glimpses of Eternitiy
*Studies in the Parables of Jesus*

A study of the parables of Jesus as compelling stories and illustrations from our familiar world which the Lord used to open windows for us into heaven. The Gospel writers shared the parables of Jesus and thus helped us to understand the heart of God and the nature of the spiritual kingdom which His Son has brought into the world at such an awful cost. There are messages of comfort in the parables and some stern warnings too. They are best understood by those who have a longing to know God's Son and to follow Him in genuine earnestness. These studies are the compilation of a series of articles written for *Christianity Magazine.* 198 pages, $12.99 (PB)

*For a full listing of DeWard Publishing
Company books, visit our website:*

**www.deward.com**

CPSIA information can be obtained
at www.ICGtesting.com
Printed in the USA
FFOW02n1046040618
46988052-49257FF